The Yoga Sūtras of Patañjali

Studies in Indian Tradition

Series Editor

Purusottama Bilimoria

Deakin University

Australia

Studies in Indian Tradition – No. 1

The Yoga Sūtras of Patañjali

An Analysis of the Sanskrit with Accompanying English Translation

by :
Christopher Chapple
Ph.D.
and
Yogi Anand Viraj
(Eugene P. Kelly Jr.)

SRI SATGURU PUBLICATIONS
A DIVISION OF
INDIAN BOOKS CENTRE
DELHI-INDIA

Published by :

© SRI SATGURU PUBLICATIONS
Indological and Oriental Publishers
A Division of
INDIAN BOOKS CENTRE
40/5, Shakti Nagar,
Delhi-110007
(INDIA)

First Edition : Delhi. 1990.

ISBN - 81-7030-244-7

Printed by :

D.K. Fine Arts Press,

Delhi.

PRINTED IN INDIA

CONTENTS

ACKNOWLEDGMENTS

The inspiration for this translation was provided by Gurāṇi Añjali, Founder and Director of Yoga Anand Ashram, Amityville, New York. Seeing the need for improved tools for the study of the yoga tradition, several of her students undertook the task for becoming educated in classical Sanskrit. In 1979, a group of us began work on the Yoga Sūtras, meeting once a week to analyze the grammar, compare different translations, and discuss the commentary of Vyāsa. The project continued in this fashion until the summer of 1986, when we completed the fourth and final section.

As with any long project, a number of people have been involved with the generation of this translation. The primary contributors to the first Pāda in addition to myself and Yogi Ananda Virāj include William Bilodeau and Yogi Ananda Satyam(Salvatore Familia). Those assisting with the translation of the second Pāda were Yogi Ananda Satyam, William Bilodeau, Roy Mitchell, and Glenn James. The third and fourth Pādas benefitted from input by Glenn James and Tom Affatigato. Kathe Jeremiah Loretta Quintano devoted long hours to typing the manuscript.

Constant support and guidance has been received from Yogi Ananda Virāj (Eugene P. Kelly, Jr.), Assistant Director of Yoga Anand Ashram. We in turn are grateful to our teachers of Sanskrit and Indian philosophy at the State University of New York at Stony Brook and Fordham University, including Antonio T. deNicolás, Alice Davison, Christopher S. George, José Pereira, and John B. Chethimattam. Most especially, we are grateful to Gurāṇi Añjali for providing the Ashram context that has made yoga a matter of the flesh, not merely an exercise of the mind.

— CC

INTRODUCTION

TECHNICAL FEATURES OF THIS TRANSLATION

This translation of the *Yoga Sūtras* is designed for those interested in making direct contact with the Sanskrit text attributed to Patañjali. Although the *Yoga Sūtras* are perhaps 2000 years more recent than the earliest Sanskrit texts of India, they are in many ways more difficult to decipher than the Vedic hymns, owing to their epigrammatic form. Each *sūtra* was designed as a mnemonic device to bring into focus specific and involved meditation practices and experiences. To explain the import of these, later scholars of yoga provided extensive written commentaries on the text including Vyāsa (fifth century C.E.), Vācaspati Miśra (ninth century C.E.), and Vijñāna Bhīkṣu (sixteenth century C.E.).

The present work is devoted to a grammatical explication of Patañjali's text accompanied by a new translation. Vyāsa and other commentators have been consulted, as well as the dozen or so English translations listed at the end.

The main contribution of this translation is to provide the reader with a comprehensive analysis of the words used by Patañjali and how they interrelate. One need know no Sanskrit in order to use this analysis. However, if one studies it carefully, a working knowledge of *sūtra* Sanskrit will be gained. With few exceptions, no verbs are used by Patañjali, immensely simplifying the task. The Romanization is given for each *sūtra*, of the text, with each word separated. Compounded words are connected with a hyphen. Then, each word is isolated and analyzed separately. Words within compounds are identified by gender; words at the end of compounds are identified by gender, grammatical case, and number. Each word is then followed by various possible translations, references to other *sūtras*, and/or a detailed analysis of prefixes and verb roots. The analysis (*vigraha*) of compounds (*samāsa*) is given in brackets at the end of the compound. Our translation of the *sūtra* then follows, sometimes accompanied with additional comments.

The single feature that most distinguishes this translation from the prior ones is that we have also used a single English word to translate Sanskrit terms, and have left a handful of terms in the Sanskrit, either because they are referring to specialized states for which there is no English equivalent (such as *guṇa, puruṣa, prakṛti, pariṇāma, saṃyama, kaivalyam*) or because the usage of a term in Sanskrit is loaded with numerous meanings, some of which would be eliminated by translation with a single term. For instance, *dharma* seems to refer to both a discrete nature and larger order of things.

In a couple of instances, we have employed terms in English that equal the Sanskrit in their elasticity. For instance, the term *viṣaya*, translated by others as "object," also is used in a more general, process-oriented sense. We have used the word "condition," which conveys both meanings. Another term for which we offer a new translation is *pratyaya*, which refers to the significance or content of a *vṛtti* or mental fluctuation. This has been rendered "presented ideas" by Woods and "knowledge" or "cause producing an effect" by Āraṇya. Drawing from the phenomenological language of Husserl and others, we have used the single word "intention," capturing the directionality that is evident in its verbal root *i* (go), prefixed with *prati* (against, toward).

The word *citta* is one of the most difficult terms to adequately translate in the *Yoga Sūtras*. Patañjali offers no definition of the term within the text. Some scholars have equated the term with the inner organ (*antaḥkaraṇa*), said in the *Sāṃkhya Kārikā* to be comprised of the intellect (*buddhi*), I-maker (*ahaṃkāra*), and mind organ (*manas*). These translators have used such terms as mind-stuff for *citta*. Others have chosen to translate the term as "consiousness." Although this may be correct etymologically (the root *cit* means "perceive"), consciousness in the India context generally refers to the pure consciousness or witnessing mode of *puruṣa*. Interestingly, *citta* can go either way. It can bind one through consciousness of things as typified in the five forms of its fluctuations (I:5-11) or it can, through its onepointedness, bring one to *sattva* and *kaivalyam* (III:55). It is through the purification of the *citta* that the nonattached state that is the goal of yoga is achieved. Because of the ambivalence of the term, the more neutral word "mind" will be used for *citta*, with *manas*, which appears only thrice, translated as mind organ.

Artha we have translated uniformally as purpose. Originally, following Vyāsa and other translators, we thought that at least two meanings pertained: in some instances *artha* seemed to refer to meaning, in other instances to objects. However, keeping in mind that all objects, as manifestations of *prakṛti*, are for the enjoyment of *puruṣa*, we have found that the word "purpose" fits consistently.

Throughout our translation we have attempted to be sensitive to various clues offered by Patañjali in the areas of style and flow that seemingly lend a greater coherence to the text than previously discerned. At variance with some earlier interpretations, we see the categorization of yogis in *Sūtra* I:22 as explicitly prescinding from the "types" described in the three prior-*sūtras*; we do not impute that Patañjali's descriptions of *Īśvara* (I:23-29) constitute a theistic stance; we interpret I:41 as providing a foundational definition for the states of *samādhi* that are later described; we see a hierarchy of subtilization evident in the descriptions of powers *(vibhūti)*, thus linking this section to Patañjali's central theme as described below; we suggest that the discernment of "two things" in III:53 might possibly refer to the perception of the distinction between the purest form of *sattva* and *puruṣa*; we see the theme of *pariṇāma* as a logical extension of his earlier statements and not an appended afterthought, as some have surmised; and, finally, we see a complementarity (if not a continuity) evident in the various descriptions of yoga that Patañjali proposes.

PATAÑJALI'S CENTRAL THEME: SUBTILIZATION

There are three principal concerns in the *Yoga Sūtra:* practice (*sādhana*), return to the origin or subtilization (*pratiprasava*), and *samādhi.* The three are interrelated and at times synchronic. The application of yogic practices causes a progressive subtilization of one's focus, which is directed away from the gross manifestations of *citta-vṛtti* to the most sublime aspect of *prakṛti,* the state of *sattva.* When this is achieved, the resulting equipoise is defined as a state where distinctions of grasped, grasping, and grasper dissolve (see I:41).

Procedurally and ultimately, yoga takes an array of approaches, offering myriad paths to the goal and several descriptions of the goal once it has been achieved. Furthermore, mention of the goal is found in each of the four sections of the text. The descriptions of each are diverse, and one could possibly choose a "favorite" description of yogic attainment whether it be jewel-like, cloud of *dharma,* or seedless. However, despite the plurality of practices and culminations, the significance of which will be discussed later, there is one matter in yoga about which there is no choice: the necessity for the practitioner to recall the *guṇas* back to a condition of equilibrium (*pratiprasava*), mentioned in II:10 and IV:34.

To understand this critical process, the link between Sāṃkhya and yoga must be acknowledged. With a few exceptions the vocabulary of yoga and Sāṃkhya is shared. Like Sāṃkhya, yoga unequivocably asserts the reality of *prakṛti.* Like Sāṃkhya, yoga extols discriminative knowledge as the means to liberation. Yoga, however, prescribes several more disciplines to achieve this elevated state and describes the results in various ways. Nonetheless, each of the disciplines of yoga serves a common purpose: to lessen attachment first to the gross world, and then to the subtle influences that shape one's perception of the gross. Ultimately, when the final state is attained, all obscurations are burned away, the *citta* is purified, and one dwells in a state of pure *sattva* that allows one to reflect pure consciousness. This *kaivalyam* or *samā dhi* is not a catatonic state nor does it require death; it is the power of higher awareness (*citi śakti*) through which one continues to observe the play of life.[1]

The technical procedure for the subtilization of the *citta* serves as a thread that binds together the *Yoga Sūtras.* This general theme has been helpful to keep in mind when our translation group encountered difficult passages. In a sense, the entire yoga system is designed to accomplish and perfect this process. It is first hinted at in the opening definition of yoga: "Yoga is the restraint of fluctuations in the mind" (I:2). It is explicitly described in the section on dispassion (I:13-16). A hierarchy of accomplishment seems to be described in I:19-22, with the mild ones ready to return to the manifestations of *prakṛti,* the medium well established in skills that keep one from bondage, and the ardent close to the vision of *puruṣa.* The progressively subtle hierarchy of concentrations (*samāpatti* and *samādhi*) given in I:44-51 (which have been commented upon extensively elsewhere). further establish the nature of yoga as requiring the gathering back of the mind from its obfuscated involvements with the world.

The beginning of the second section (*Sādhana-pāda*) of the text clearly outlines that which is to be overcome by the practice of yoga. The fluctuations of the mind, inextricably linked to karma and the afflictions, are to be avoided through meditation (II:11), which returns the practitioner to a state of equilibrium. The discriminating one sees the dissatisfaction (*duḥkha*) inherent in worldly involvement (II:15) and seeks to avoid the dissatisfaction of the future (II:16) through understanding the world-generating process of the seen (II:18). Once it is seen that all activity is only performed for the sake of the seer, then it is in fact called back to its origin, reminiscent of the *Sāṃkhya Kārikā* when *prakṛto* ceases her dance. At this point, the culmination of the subtilization process, a state of wisdom is achieved: "From following the limbs of yoga, on the destruction of impurity there is a light of knowledge, leading to discriminative discernment" (II:28).

The eightfold yoga path, described in II:29 through III:3, similarly follows a process of increasing subtilization. The first phase, *yama,* involves a conscious displacement of the habits of violence, lying, stealing, lust, and possessiveness. Each of these involves turning away from attachment to the gross. Next, in the practice of *niyama,* one cultivates new interactions in the world based on purity, contentment, austerity, self-study, and dedication to *Īśvara.*

Having thus stabilized one's social intercourse, one then focuses directly on the outer layer of one's immediate self, the body. Through *āsana,* comfort and steadiness are gained (II:46); through breath control, the internal and external conditions of breath are transcended (II:51). This then allows, in the final four phases of yoga, the taking on of the most subtle aspects of the *citta.* The first of these four, *pratyāhāra,* specifically is defined as the withdrawal from objects of sense; it is followed by the inner limbs of concentration, meditation, and *samādhi,* which are taken up in the third section of the text.

Throughout the third section (*Vibhūti-pāda*), the powers resulting from progressive subtilization are detailed. All are seen to stem from a mind that is disciplined by the inner limbs of concentration, meditation, and *samādhi,* a mind that is no longer directed to the outer world (see III:9-11). Numerous skills arise, but none are necessarily seen by another (III:20) because the transformation takes place within the experience of the yogin.

Some of the more fantastic *sūtras* in this section can perhaps be reread in light of the subtilization process. For instance, the discussion in III:39-41 implies the ascension through the *tattvas* advocated in Sāṃkhya. The yogin is first able to rise above the grossest elements of water and mud (III:39) and through fire (III:40) using the breath (air) to the subtlest of elements, space (II:41). *Sūtra* III:44 summarizes the initial attainment of mastery over the elements, stating their dependence on that which is more subtle; III:47 takes this a stage higher, stating that mastery of the sense organs is gained by knowledge of the sense of self. Yet even higher than this, again following the course of *pratiprasava*, a steady, dispassionate vision, *(kaivalyam)* is revealed. This progression, from mastery of the elements, to mastery of the senses, to mastery of the mind, and finally, the stilling of the mind, reaffirms the emphasis placed by Patañjali on subtilization, a concern also found in the *Bhagavad Gītā*: "The senses are great, they say, but the mind is above the senses, and intellect above the mind. And above the intellect is He" (II:42).

The fourth section (*Kaivalya-pāda*) continues the theme of return to the origin, again using a highly Sāṃkhyan terminology. The concept of the *pariṇāma* of *citta* is central in Paṭañjali's presentation here. It had been established in III:9-15 that the *pariṇāma* or transformation of the *citta* can either be directed outward toward manifestation (III:13) or called back to the point of restraint or *nirodha* (III:9), which, when applied consistently, leads to the *parināma* of *samādhi* (III:11). In the fourth section, again we find the same themes echoed. Things arise because of the stabilization of *pariṇāma* (IV:2,14); the goal of yoga is the reversal of this process, the conclusion of *pariṇāma* (IV:32,33) wherein the compulsive generation of the world ceases.

In his interpretation of the discussion of *citta* and *pariṇāma* in the fourth section, Vyāsa interprets Patañjali as arguing against the Buddhist Yogācāra school, which has been seen by some as a pure idealism, negating the reality of the manifest world. However, in our reading of the text, we do not see Patañjali explicitly polemicizing against such a view, but merely advancing the Sāṃkhya perspective that all things stem from *prakṛti* through *pariṇāma*; that *pariṇāma* can be directed to increasingly subtle levels through *pratiprasava*, and that the culmination of this process results in the total purification of the *citta*. This yields a state of *sattva* that is characterized as higher awareness, steadfastness in own form, *kaivalyam* (III:34).

As in Sāṃkhya, it is noted that *prakṛti* cannot operate without *puruṣa* (IV:3); it needs a witness for whom to perform. The performance is played out through a mistaken self identity (IV:4) but is only possible because of the unchanging witness (IV:18). Both are necessary; neither is sufficient unto itself, as stated in the Sāṃkhya analogy of the lame assisting the blind. Though they work together, they remain essentially separate.

Despite any attempts to limit or claim the power of consciousness by way of identification, the Self can never be seen (IV:21). It is only through the suspension of all identification by the process of *pratiprasava* that *kaivalyam* takes place. The process of identification is inseparable from that of afflicted action; identity is the second of the five afflictions that bind one to action. Both stem from residues in the *citta* that cause repeated manifestation. The explanation of karma in this section (IV:7-11) asserts that experience is dependent on the *citta's* structures. When the mind is returned to its origin in *prakṛti*, and when highest *sattva* is achieved (IV:25), the generation of the false sense of self ceases. This purity guarantees nonafflicted action (IV:30), with the culmination of yoga given in the final *sūtra* as:

> The return to the origin of the *guṇas*,
> emptied of their purpose for *puruṣa*,
> is *kaivalyam*, the steadfastness in own form,
> and the power of higher awareness.

SOME OBSERVATIONS ON THE STRUCTURE OF THE TEXT

Having examined the thread that in our reading binds the text together, we will now note those aspects of the text that scholars have found particularly noncohesive. These issues may be divided as follows: 1) the date of the text 2) the plurality of practices included 3) the various descriptions of the goal 4) the presence of Buddhist and Jaina elements 5) the position of some that there are are multiple texts contained in the *Yoga Sūtras.*

First, let us begin with the dating of the text. Two contemporary scholars of yoga vary by as much as five hundred years in their placing of the date. Georg Feuerstein claims it "is a product of the third century A.D."[2] while T. S. Rukmani, following S. N. Dasgupta, states that the date "can be accepted as between the second century B.C. and the first century A.D."[3] thus allowing for a possible identification between the composer of the *Yoga Sūtra* and the grammarian of the same name. The early scholars Jacobi, Keith, and Poussin assent to the later date; Dasgupta thinks the first three sections were early, and that the last one is a later accretion.[4] From our reading of the text as noted earlier in this introduction in our discussion of subtilization, we see a continuity throughout. However, for reasons detailed below, we would support the notion that Patañjali flourished after the popularization of various yogic techniques practiced by diverse schools, Buddhist, Brahmanical, and Jaina. As Eliade has stated, "they are not his discoveries, not those of his time; they had been first tested many centuries before him."[5]

The methods of practice taught by Patañjali are extensive and various. More than twenty different techniques can be itemized, many of which may be subdivided into component parts. The first method mentioned by Patañjali is practice and dispassion (*abhyāsa* and *vairāgya* [I:12-16]). Another is to apply faith, energy, mindfulness, concentration, and wisdom (*śraddhā, vīrya, smṛti, samādhi, prajñā* [I:20]). Yet another is to dedicate one's meditation to the primal teacher, *īśvara*, who remains untainted by the ravages of change inflicted by association with *prakṛti* [I:23-32; II:1, 32,45]. Appropriate behavior in interpersonal relationships is seen to be another tool for achieving yoga: *Sūtra* I:33 states: "One should cultivate friendship with the joyful, compassion for the sorrowful, gladness for those who are virtuous, and equanimity in regard to the non virtuous; through this, the mind is pacified." In gaining control over the breath, the yogin masters the senses, including the thinking process [I:34; II:49-53]. Other practices in the first *pāda* include directing one's consciousness to one who has conquered attachment, or meditating on an auspicious dream experience, or centering the mind in activity, or cultivating thoughts which are sorrowless and illuminating, or by any other means, as desired [I:35-39].

In the second *pāda*, two main forms of practice are prescribed, each containing multiple dimensions. The first, *Kriyā Yoga*, involves austerity, self-study, and dedication to *īśvara* with the express purpose of uprooting the influence of impurity (*kleśa*) [II: -27]. The second, *Aṣṭānga Yoga*, contains the well-known eight limbs of yoga, each of which may be considered as a distinct form of practice: *yama, niyama, āsana, prāṇāyāma, pratyāhāra, dhāraṇā, dhyāna, samādhi.* [II:28-III:3].

In addition to the plurality of practices mentioned in the *Yoga Sūtras*, yoga is described in various places throughout the text with often quite variant characteristics. In the first section, it is described as "restraint of the fluctuations of the mind" (I:2), as "a jewel assuming the color of any near object, with unity among grasper, grasping, and grasped" (I:41), as "clarity of authentic self" (I:47) and as "seedless" (I:51). In the second section, it is described as the disappearance of the seen (II:21,22), leaving the pure seer (II:20). Mention is made in the third section of the purity of *sattva* as equal to that of the *puruṣa* (III:35, 49, 55), which is said to be the same as *kaivalyam*. And in the fourth and final section, several descriptions of yogic attainments are found: "discriminative discernment" and "cloud of *dharma samādhi*" (IV:29), "cessation of afflicted action" (IV:30), "the end of *parniṇāma* (IV:33), and "the return to the origin of the *guṇas*" "steadfastness in own form," and "power of higher awareness" (IV:34). As is evident, concern for the culmination of yoga pervades the text; this is not a narrative where the climax is saved and not revealed until the conclusion. Furthermore, it is difficult to reconcile the technically precise requirement that all things be restrained (*nirodha*) with the more poetic proclamations of cloud of *dharma samādhi* and higher awareness (*citi śakti*). Are these competing goals or different descriptions of the same experience? Are they contradictory? Or perhaps, as we will explore at the end of this introduction, Patañjali has purposefully presented an artful array of possibilities.

Traces of both Buddhism and Jainism are found in the *Yoga Sūtras*. Many of the practices mentioned in the *Yoga Sūtras* undoubtedly have their roots in the classical Hindu, specifically Upaniṣadic-Brahmanical tradition, reflecting prescriptions from the *Kaṭha* and *Śvetāśvatara Upaniṣads*, the *Mahābhārata*, and other texts. However, while retaining its Sāṃkhya-oriented philosophical position, the *Yoga Sūtras* do incorporate practices which must have been identifiably associated with Buddhism and Jainism at the time of Patañjali. Several scholars have pointed out the parallels between Buddhist Yoga and the yoga of Patañjali, including Senart, Lindquist, la Vallée Poussin, Eliade, and others. Eliade accepts Senart's assessment that Buddhism arose "on the terrain of yoga."[6] However, this "terrain" must refer to the pre-Patañjali prototradition, probably older than any institutionalized religion for which we have historical records, since the earliest date which scholars have advanced for the *Yoga Sūtras* is 200 B.C. to 100 A.D., and even later, post-dating Buddhism by at least three and possibly eight centuries.

The parallels cited by Poussin and others are so pervasive in Buddhist literature and so absent from the traditional "Hindu" literature, that it cannot be denied that Patañjali chose to include yogic practices from Buddhist manuals. The most obvious of these include the five practices listed in I:20 of *śraddhā, vīrya, smṛti, samādhi, prajñā*; the four *brahmavihara* widely applied by Buddhists cited in *sūtra* I:33, and the parallel definitions of ignorance (*avidyā*) and suffering (*duḥkha*) in II:5 and II:15, respectively. Similarities can also be seen between the four *dhyānas* in Buddhism and the *Samādhis* listed by Patañjali, the reference to seven *prajñas* [II:27], and so forth.[7] Keith even goes so far as to state that "it is only the light of the Mahāyāna (Buddhist) doctrine of '*tathāgatagarbha* and the Yogācāra use of the term *bīja* in this connection, that we can understand the statement of *īśvara* in *Yoga Sūtra* I:25: "In him the germ of the omniscient reaches its highest state!"[8]

The scholarship about the relationship between Buddhism and the *Yoga Sūtras* has been extensive. Less attention has been given to Jaina influence in the various analytical studies of the text. Three teachings closely associated with Jainism appear in Yoga: the doctrine of *karma*, the *telos* of isolation (*kevala* in Jainism, *kaivalyam* in Yoga), and the practice of nonviolence (*ahiṃsā*). In fact, the entire list of the five *yamas* (II:30) is identical with the ethical precepts taught by Mahāvira, the contemporary of the Buddha who established the foundations of modern Jainism.

The various pieces of evidence given above have caused modern Western scholars to speculate that the text as it now appears is in fact a patchwork. The absence of a perceived architectonic has led to many attempts to dissect the text into the original sections that had been sewn together by Patañjali. The most recent attempt, by Georg Feuerstein, sees two yogic texts melded together:a "Kriyā Yoga Text" extending from I:1 to II:27 and from III:3 or 4 to IV:34, interrupted by an "Aṣṭāṅga Yoga Text" which extends from II:28 to III:2 or 3 and also picks up *sūtra* III:55. Hence, he would include all the practices of the first *pāda* as part of *kriyā yoga*, along with the discussion of *kaivalyam* in the fourth *pāda*.[9] Deussen claims that the *Yoga Sūtra* was patched together from five different texts, dividing the first *pāda* into two sections, isolating the *Kriyā Yoga* section of the second *pāda*, extending *Aṣṭāṅga Yoga* through the third *pāda*, and regarding the *Kaivalyam Pāda* as an independent text.[10] Hauer similarly postulates five texts, which he dubs *Nirodha* [I:1-22], *Īśvarapraṇidhā na* [I:23-51], *Kriyā-yoga* [II:1-27], *Yoga-aṅga* [II:28-III:55], and *Nirmāṇa-citta* [IV:1-34].[11] Frauwallner sees a distinctive difference between the *nirodha* form of yoga described in *pāda* one which he claims calls for the suppression of "every mental activity" and the Eight-limbed Yoga of *pāda* two, which, he asserts, "seeks to raise the capacity for knowledge to the highest."[12] Dasgupta, however, remains unperturbed by what might be considered inconsistencies in the text, referring to it as a "masterly and systematic compilation."[13] In any case, it is clear from purely internal evidence that the text involves the overlay and interweaving of various yogic traditions which became harmonized not by inherent consistency but through their joint appearance through Patañjali.

At this juncture, I wish to turn to a discussion of the methodology employed by Patañjali. We have seen that the *Yoga Sūtras* consist of a concatenation of distinct schools of yoga which can be variously designated as *nirodha yoga, samādhi yoga, kriyā yoga, aṣṭāṅga yoga*, along with practices drawn from the Buddhists, Jainas, and perhaps others. However, I hesitate to describe Patañjali's process with the term syncretism, defined by Berling as a "borrowing, affirmation, or integration of concepts, symbols or practices of one religious tradition into another by a process of selection and reconciliation."[14] Patañjali simply does not reconcile or mathematically "total out" the diverse practices he mentions; as Frauwallner has written, "The *Yoga Sūtra* of Patañjali is composed of different constituents or elements which, in no way, give a uniform homogeneous picture."[15] However, the text has been immensely successful, surviving nearly two millenia.

To understand Patañjali's success, we must keep in mind that the text is one not of positions but of practices. Furthermore, the *telos* of the various practices, whether described as *nirodha*, *kaivalyam*, or *samādhi*, lies beyond language, beyond intellectual speculation: and this experience, which is itself beyond syncretism or synthesis, holds the text together. The text has meaning in that its practice obliterates all meaning. Patañjali has no point to prove; he does not advance one practice above another. The practice which is effective is the one to be used, as indicated in *Sūtra* II:39, *yathā abhimata dhyānād vā* (or from meditation as desired). Patañjali provides us with an important clue regarding his method in the first *pāda*. When listing all the practices to be undertaken, he uses the connecting particle *vā* (or), not *ca* (and). Just as the terms "wave" and "particle" are both used to describe an electron, vascillating according to context, so the practices and attainments expounded by Patañjali stand in juxtaposition and in complementarity; although they all seek to bring about yogic experience, they cannot be said to be identical.

This method is similar to that employed in the *Bhagavad Gītā* where again and again Arjuna asks Krishna for one truth and again and again Krishna offers Arjuna yet another perspective, another chapter, another yoga. Each view, whether that of a god being sacrificed to or a yogic discipline being practiced, is given life as long as it proves effective. Multiplicity is the rule. without one perspective, one god, or one yoga gaining ascendency. The culmination of yoga comes when all differentiations are obliterated in *nirodha* or *samādhi*. This is not to say that all life ends, but that a state of being is attained wherein, paraphrasing *Sūtra* I:41, "like a clear jewel, one has unity among the grasper, grasping, and grasped," a state of yoga wherein totality is embraced without denying multiplicity.

Contradictions are seemingly present in the *Yoga Sūtra* of Patañjali; it undoubtedly would not withstand the consistency test of a modern analytic philosopher. However, the method used by Patañjali seems to reflect some of the central concerns of the system itself. Various paths are announced, but judgments are not pronounced; no teaching is said to be higher or better. Differences between the various systems of practice are not denied, nor are they even discussed. The method by which Patañjali presents the various yogas is consistent with their goal as if having himself become established in ***kaivalyam,*** he surveys them with a dispassionate eye, seeing the possibility of each. His techniques coexist in complementarity, not competition. Some have said that Patañjali has made no specific philosophical contribution in his presentation of the yoga school. To the contrary, I suggest that his is a masterful contribution communicated through nonjudgmentally presenting diverse practices, a methodology deeply rooted in the culture and traditions of India.

Christopher Chapple
Loyola Marymount University,

Los Angeles, California, U.S.A.

NOTES

1. See Christopher Chapple, "*Citta-vṛtti* and Reality in the *Yoga Sūtra*" in *Sāṃkhya-Yoga : Proceedings of the IASWR Conference, 1981* (Stony Brook, New York: The Institute for Advanced Studies of World Religions, 1983), pp. 103-119.
2. Georg Feuerstein, *The Yoga Sūtra of Patañjali: A New Translation and Commentary* (Folkestone: Dawson, 1979), p.3.
3. T.S. Rukmani, *Yogavārttika of Vijñānabhikṣu, Samādhipāda* (Delhi: Munshiram Manoharlal, 1981), p. 3:
4. For a summary of the views of these and others, see Mircea Eliade, *Yoga: Immortality and Freedom* (Princeton: Princeton University Press, 1969), pp. 370-372.
5. Ibid., p. 9.
6. Mircea Eliade, *Yoga: Immortality and Freedom* (Princeton University Press, 1969), p. 162. See also Emile Senart, "Bouddhisme et Yoga" in *La Revue de l'histoire des relgious,* Vol. XLII (1900), pp. 345-364.
7. Louis de la Vallée Poussin, "Le Bouddhisme et le Yoga de Patañjali" in *mélanges chinois et bouddhiques,* Vol. V (1936-37), pp. 232-242.
8. A.B. Keith, *Indian Historical Quarterly,* Vol. III(1932), p. 434, as quoted in la Vallée Poussin, ibid.
9. Georg Feuerstein, *The Yoga Sūtra of Patañjali: An Exercise in the Methodology of Textual Analysis* (New Delhi: Arnold Heinemann, 1979), pp. 87-88.
10. Paul Deussen, *Allgemeine Geschichte der Philosophie,* Vol. I, Pt. 3, Leipzig, 1920, (as summarized in Feuerstein, *ibid.,* p. 37).
11. J.W. Hauer, *Der Yoga,* Stuttgart, 1958 (as summarized in Feuerstein, *ibid.,* p. 42).

12. Erich Frauwallner, *History of Indian Philosophy,* Vol. I, tr. by V.M. Bedekar (Delhi: Motilal Banarsidass, 1973), pp. 344-345.
13. S.N. Dasgupta, *Yoga Philosophy in Relation to Other Systems of Indian Thought* (University of Calcutta, 1951), p. 51.
14. Judith A. Berling, *The Syncretic Religion of Lin Chao-en* (New York: Columbia University Press, 1980), p. 9.
15. Frauwallner, op. cit., p. 335.

The *Yoga Sūtras* of Patañjali: Continuous Translation

I: Samādhi Pāda

1. Now, instruction in yoga.
2. Yoga is the restraint of fluctuations in the mind.
3. Then there is abiding in the seer's own from.
4. At other times it takes the form of the fluctuations.
5. The fluctuations are fivefold, afflicted or nonafflicted.
6. Valid cognition, error conceptualization, sleep, and memory.
7. Valid cognitions are perception, inference, and valid testimony.
8. Error is false knowledge, without foundation in form.
9. Conceptualization is the result of words and ideas empty of objects.
10. The sleep fluctuation is based on the intention of nonbecoming.
11. Memory is the recollection of an experienced condition.
12. Through practice and dispassion arises restraint.
13. Effort in remaining there is practice.
14. But that is firmly situated when carefully attended to for a long time without interruption.
15. Dispassion is the knowledge of mastery in one who thirsts not for conditions seen or heard.
16. That highest (dispassion)--thirstlessness for the *guṇas* -- [proceeds] from the discernment of *puruṣa.*
17. *Samprajñāta* arises from association with discursive thought, reflection, bliss, and I-am-ness.
18. The other [state] has *saṃskāra* only and is preceded by practice and the intention of cessation.
19. Of the ones who are absorbed in *prakṛti* and discarnate, there

is an intention of becoming.

20. Of the others it is preceded by faith, energy, mindfulness, *samādhi,* and wisdom.

21. The strongly intense ones are near.

22. Hence the distinctions of mild, moderate, and ardent.

23. Or from dedication to *Īśvara.*

24. *Īśvara* is a distinct *puruṣa* untouched by afflictions, actions, fruitions, or their residue.

25. There the seed of omniscience is unsurpassed.

26. Due to its being unlimited by time, it is the teacher of the prior ones.

27. Its expression is *praṇava (OM).*

28. Repetition of it and realization of its purpose [should be made].

29. Thus inward-consciousness is attained and obstacles do not arise.

30. These obstacles, distractions of the mind, are: sickness, dullness, doubt, carelessness, laziness, sense addition, false view, nonattainment of a stage, and instability.

31. A dissatisfied, despairing body and unsteady inhalation and exhalation accompany the distractions.

32. For the purpose of counteracting them, there is the practice of one thing (*eka tattva*).

33. Clarification of the mind [results] from the cultivation of friendliness, compassion, happiness, and equanimity in conditions of pleasure, dissatisfaction, merit, and absence of merit, respectively.

34. Or by expulsion and retention of breath.

35. Or steady binding of the mind organ arises in the activity of involvement with a condition.

36. Or having sorrowless illumination.

37. Or [on a] mind in a condition free from attachment.

38. Or resting on knowledge [derived] from dream or sleep.

39. Or from meditation as desired.

40. Mastery of it [extends] from the smallest to the greatest.

41. [The accomplished mind] of diminished fluctuations, like a precious (or clear) jewel assuming the color of any near object, has unity among grasper, grasping, and grasped.

42. *Savitarkā* unity is the commingling by conceptualization of word, purpose, and knowledge.

43. *Nirvitarkā* is when memory is purified, as if emptied of its own form, and the purpose alone shines forth.

44. Similarly explained are *savicāra* and *nirvicāra* which are sutle conditions.

45. And the subtle condition terminates in the undesignated.

46. These are *samādhi* with seed.

47. In skill with *nirvicāra*, clarity of authentic self arises.

48. There the wisdom is *ṛtaṃ* bearing.

49. Its condition is different from heard or inferred knowledge because of its distinct purpose.

50. The *saṃskāra* born of it obstructs other *saṃskāras*.

51. With even that restricted, everything is restricted and that is seedless *samādhi*.

II:Sādhana Pāda

1. Austerity, self-study ,and dedication to *Īśvara* are *kriyā-yoga*.

2. [It is] for the purposes of cultivating *samādhi* and attenuating the afflictions.

3. Ignorance, I-am-ness, attraction, aversion, and desire for con-

tinuity are the afflictions.

4. Ignorance is the origin of the others, whether dormant, attenuated, interrupted, or fully active.

5. Ignorance is seeing the noneternal as eternal, the impure as pure, dissatisfaction as pleasure, and the nonself as self.

6. I-am-ness is when the two powers of seer and seen [appear] as a single self.

7. Attraction is clinging to pleasure.

8. Aversion is clinging to dissatisfaction.

9. Desire for continuity, arising even among the wise, is sustained by self-inclination.

10. These subtle ones are to be avoided by a return to the origin.

11. Their fluctuations are to be avoided by meditation.

12. The residue of karma, rooted in affliction, is felt in seen or unseen existence.

13. While the root exists, there is fruition of it as birth, duration, and experience.

14. These fruits are joyful or painful according to whether the causes are meritorious or demeritorious.

15. For the discriminating one, all is dissatisfaction, due to the conflict of the fluctuations of the *guṇas* and by the dissatisfactions due to *parniṇāma*, sorrow, and *saṃskāra*.

16. The dissatisfaction yet to come is to be avoided.

17. The cause of what is to be avoided is the union of seer with the seen.

18. The seen has the qualities of light, activity, and inertia, consists of the elements and the senses, and has the purposes of experience and liberation.

19. The distinct, the indistinct, the designator, and the unmanifest are the divisions of the *guṇas.*

20. The seer only sees; though pure, it appears intentional.

21. The nature of the seen is only for the purpose of that (*puruṣa*).

22. When [its] purpose is done, it disappears; otherwise it does not disappear due to being common to others.

23. Union (*saṃyoga*) is the cause of apprehending as [one] self-form the two powers of owner and owned.

24. The cause of it is ignorance.

25. From its absence, *saṃyoga* ceases; [this is] the escape, the isolation from the seen.

26. The means of escape is unfaltering discriminative discernment.

27. His wisdom to the last stage is sevenfold.

28. From following the limbs of yoga, on the destruction of impurity there is a light of knowledge, leading to discrimina tive discernment.

29. Restraint, observances, postures, control of breath, withdrawal, concentration, meditation, and *samādhi* are the eight limbs.

30. The restraints are nonviolence, truthfulness, nonstealing, sexual restraint, and nonpossession.

31. When not limited by life-state, place, time, or circumstance in all occasions [these constitute] the great vow.

32. Purity, contentment, austerity, self-study, and dedication to *Īśvara* are the observances.

33. When there is bondage due to discursive thought, the cultivation of the opposite [is prescribed].

34. Discursive thoughts like violence, etc., whether done, caused, or approved, consisting in lust, anger, or delusion, and whether mild, medium, or intense, have as their endless fruits and ignorance; thus, cultivation of opposites [is prescribed].

35. When in the presence of one established in nonviolence, there is the abandonment of hostility.

36. When established in truthfulness, [there is] correspondence between action and fruit.

37. When established in nonstealing, [whatever is] present is all jewels.

38. When established in sexual restraint, vigor is obtained.

39. When steadfast in nonpossession, there is knowledge of "the how" of existence.

40. From purity arises dislike for one's own body and noncontact with others.

41. And purity of *sattva* cheerfulness, onepointedness, mastery of the senses, and fitness for the vision of the self.

42. From contentment, unsurpassed happiness is obtained.

43. From austerity arises the destruction of impurity and the perfection of the body and the senses.

44. From self-study arises union with the desired deity.

45. Perfection in *samādhi* [arises] from dedication to *Īśvara*.

46. *Āsana* is steadiness and ease,

47. From relaxation of effort and endless unity.

48. Thus, there is no assault by the pairs of opposites.

49. Being in this, there is control of breath, which is the cutting off of the motion of inbreath and outbreath.

50. Its fluctuations are external, internal, and suppressed; it is

observed according to time, place, and number, and becomes long and subtle.

51. The fourth is withdrawal from external and internal conditions [of breath].

52. Thus, the covering of light is dissolved.

53. And there is fitness of the mind organ for concentrations.

54. Withdrawal of the senses is the disengagement from conditions as if in imitation of the own-form of the mind.

55. Then arises utmost command of the senses.

III: Vibhūti Pāda

1. Concentration of the mind is [its] bondage to a place.
2. The extension of one intention there is meditation.
3. When the purpose alone shines forth as if empty of own form, that indeed is *samādhi*.
4. The unity of these three is *saṃyama*.
5. From the mastery of that, the splendor of wisdom.
6. Its application is in stages.
7. These three inner limbs are [distinct] from the prior ones.
8. These are indeed outer limbs [in regard] to the seedless.
9. [In regard to] the two *saṃskāras* of emergence and restraint, when that of appearance (emergence) is overpowered, there follows a moment of restraint in the mind; this is the *pariṇā ma* of restraint.
10. From the *saṃskāras* of this there is a calm flow.
11. When there is destruction of all objectivity and the arising of onepointedness, there is of the mind the *pariṇāma* of *samādhi*.
12. Hence again, when there is equality between arising and

quieted intentions. there is the *pariṇāma* of onepointedness of the mind.

13. By this are similarly explained the *pariṇāmas* of stability, designation, and *dharma* amongst the elements and the senses.

14. The *dharma* holder corresponds to the *dharma* whether quieted, arisen or undetermined (past, present, or future).

15. The cause of the difference between *pariṇāmas* is the difference in the succession.

16. From *saṃyama* on the threefold *pariṇāmas* there is knowledge of past and future.

17. From the overlapping here and there of words, purposes, and intentions, there is confusion. From *saṃyama* on the distinctions of them, there is knowledge of the [way of] utterance of all beings.

18. From effecting the perception of *saṃskāra*, there is knowledge of previous births.

19. [Similarly, from perception of another's] intention, there is knowledge of another mind.

20. But this is not with support because there is no condition of it in the elements.

21. From *saṃyama* on the form of the body, there arises the suspension of the power of what is to be grasped and the disjunc tion of light and the eye, resulting in concealment.

22. Karma is either in motion or not in motion. From *saṃyama* on this, or from natural phenomena boding misfortune, there is knowledge of death.

23. [By *saṃyama*] on friendliness and so forth, [corresponding] powers.

24. [By *saṃyama*] on powers, the powers like those of an

elephant, and so forth.

25. Due to the casting of light on a [sense] activity, there is knowledge of the subtle, concealed, and distant.

26. From *saṃyama* on the sun [arises] knowledge of the world.

27. On the moon, knowledge of the ordering of the stars.

28. On the polar star, knowledge of their movement.

29. On the central *cakra*, knowledge of the ordering of the body.

30. On the hollow of the throat, cessation of hunger and thirst.

31. On the tortoise *nāḍī*, stability.

32. On the light in the head, vision of perfected ones.

33. Or from intuition, everything.

34. On the heart, understanding of the mind.

35. When there is no distinction of intention between the pure *puruṣa* and the perfect *sattva*, there is experience for the purpose of the other (*puruṣa*); from *saṃyama* on purpose being for the self, there is knowledge of *puruṣa*.

36. Hence are born intuitive hearing, touching, seeing, tasting, and smelling.

37. These are impediments to *samādhi*; in emergence (world production), they are perfections.

38. From the relaxation of the cause of bondage and from the perception of a manifestation, there is an entering of the mind into another embodiment.

39. From mastery of the upbreath, there is nonattachment amongst water, mud, thorns, etc., and a rising above.

40. From mastery of the *samāna*, there is radiance.

41. From *saṃyama* on the connection between the ear and space, [there arises] the divine ear.

42. From *saṃyama* on the connection between the body and space, and from unity with the lightness of cotton, there is movement through space.

43. An outer, genuine fluctuation is the great discarnate; hence, the covering of light is destroyed.

44. From *saṃyana* on the significance and connection of the subtle and the own-form of the gross, there is mastery over the elements.

45. Hence arise the appearance of minuteness and so forth, perfection of the body, and unassailability of its *dharma*.

46. Perfection of the body is beauty of form, strength, and adamantine stability.

47. From *saṃyama*, on form, grasping I-am-ness, their connection and their significance, there is mastery over the sense organs.

48. Hence, there is swiftness of the mind organ, a state of being beyond the senses, and mastery over the *pradhāna*.

49. Only from the discernment of the difference between *sattva* and *puruṣa*, there is sovereignty over all states of being and knowledge of all.

50. From dispassion toward even this, in the destruction of the seed of this impediment, arises *kaivalyam*.

51. There is no cause for attachment and pride upon the invitation of those well established, because of repeated association with the undesirable.

52. From *saṃyama* on the moment and its succession, there is knowledge born of discrimination.

53. Hence there is the ascertainment of those two things that are

similar, due to their not being limited by difference of birth, designation, and place.

54. The knowledge born of discrimination is said to be liberating, [inclusive of] all conditions and all times, and nonsuccessive.

55. In the sameness of purity between the *sattva* and the *puruṣa*, there is *kaivalyam.*

IV: Kaivalya Pāda

1. Perfections are born due to birth, drugs, *mantra*, austerity, or *samādhi.*

2. From the flooding of *prakṛti* arises *pariṇāma* into other life states.

3. Hence, [those things that] divide the limitations of these manifestations are the instrumental cause, not the initiator, as in the case of the farmer (who does not initiate the flow of water but directs it through the use of barriers).

4. The fabricating minds states arise only from I-am-ness.

5. The initiator is the one mind among many that is distinct from activity.

6. There, what is born of meditation is without residue.

7. The action of a yogin is neither white nor black; that of others is threefold.

8. Hence, the manifestation of habit patterns thus corresponds to the fruition of that (karma).

9. Because memory and *saṃskāra* are of one form, there is a link even among births, places, and times that are concealed.

10. And there is no beginning of these due to the perpetuity of desire.

11. Because they are held together by causes, results, correspon-

dences, and supports, when these [go into] nonbeing, [there is the] nonbeing of the them (*saṃskāras*).

12. In their own form, the past and future exist, due to distinctions between paths of *dharmas*.
13. These have manifest and subtle *guṇa* natures.
14. From the uniformity of its *pariṇāma*, there is the "thatness" of an object.
15. In the sameness of an object, because of its distinctness from the mind, there is a separate path of each.
16. An object does not depend on one mind; there is no proof of this: how could it be?
17. An object of the mind is known or not known, due to the anticipation that colors it (the mind).
18. The fluctuations of the mind are always known due to the changelessness of their master, *puruṣa*.
19. There is no self-luminosity of that (*citta-vṛtti*) because of the nature of the seen.
20. In one circumstance, there is no ascertainment of both (together).
21. In the seeing of another mind there is an overstretching of the intellect from the intellect and a confusion of memory.
22. Due to the non mixing of higher awareness, entering into that form is [in fact] the perception of one's own intellect.
23. All purposes [are known due to] the mind being tinted with seer and seen.
24. From action having been done conjointly for the purpose of another, it is speckled with innumerable habit patterns.
25. The one who sees the distinction discontinues the cultivation of self-becoming.

26. Then, inclined toward discrimination, the mind has a propensity for *kaivalyam.*

27. In the intervening spaces of that, there are other intentions, due to *saṃskāras.*

28. The cessation of them is said to be like that of the afflictions.

29. Indeed, in [that state of] reflection, for the one who has discriminative discernment and always takes no interest, there is the cloud of *dharma samādhi.*

30. From that, there is cessation of afflicted action.

31. Then, little is to be known due to the eternality of knowledge which is free from all impure covering.

32. From that, the purpose of the *guṇas* is done and the succession of *pariṇāma* is concluded.

33. Succession and its correlate, the moment, are terminated by the end of *pariṇāma.*

34. The return to the origin of the *guṇas*, emptied of their purpose for *puruṣa*, is *kaivalyam*, the steadfastness in own form, and the power of higher awareness.

GRAMMATICAL ABBREVIATIONS

abl.	ablative case
adj.	adjective
acc.	accusative case
adv.	adverb
BV cpd.	*bahuvṛhi samāsa* (descriptive compound)
du.	dual
DV cpd.	*dvandva samāsa* (copulative compound)
f.	feminine
gen.	genitive case
ind.	indeclinable
instr.	instrumental case
KD cpd.	*karmadharya samāsa* (adjectival compound)
loc.	locative case
m.	masculine
n.	neuter
nom.	nominative case
pl.	plural
p.p.p.	past passive participle
pron.	pronoun
sg.	singular
TP cpd.	*tat puruṣa samāsa* (compound which indicates case relationship between members, generally followed by Sanskrit case number [see below])

Grammatical cases:

1. nominative
2. accusative
3. instrumental
4. dative
5. ablative
6. genitive
7. locative

I. Samādhi Pāda

1. *atha yoga-anuśāsanam*

***atha* (adv.) now**

yoga* (m.) union, connection, joining; from √*yuj
(unite, join, connect, employ, use)

anuśāsanam (n. nom. sg.) instruction, direction, teaching; *anu* (after, with) + *śāsana*, from √*śas* (chastise, correct, restrain, teach) [end of TP7 cpd.]

Now, instruction in yoga.

2. *yogaś citta-vṛtti-nirodhaḥ*

yogaś (m. nom. sg.) yoga (see above)

citta (n.) mind. reason, intelligence ; from √*cit* (perceive, observe, know)

vṛtti (f.) modification, turning, fluctuations; from √*vṛt* (turn, revolve, roll, move) [end of TP6 cpd.]

nirodhaḥ (m. nom. sg.) restraint, control, suppression; *ni* (down, into) + *rodha*, from √*rudh* (obstruct, arrest, avert) [end of TP6 cpd.]

Yoga is the restraint of fluctuations of the mind.

3. *tadā draṣṭuḥ sva rūpe'vasthānam*

tadā (ind.) then

draṣṭuḥ (m. gen. sg.) of the seer; from √*dṛś* (see, perceive, understand)

svarūpe (n. loc. sg.) in own form; *sva* (own, self) + *rūpa* (form, shape, figure)

avasthānam (n. nom. sg.) abiding, standing, dwelling; *ava* (off, away) + *sthāna*, from √*sthā* (stand, endure, continue)

Then there is abiding in the seer's own form.

4. *vṛtti-sārūpyam itaratra*

vṛtti (f.) fluctuation (see I.2)
sārūpyam (n. nom. sg.) with the form, likeness, similarity of form; *sā* (with) + *rūpya* (stamped, impressions in the possession of), from *rūpa* (see I.3) [end of TP6 cpd.]
itaratra (ind.) at other times, otherwise

At other times it takes the form of the fluctuations.

5. *vṛttayaḥ pañcatayaḥ kliṣṭa-akliṣṭāḥ*
vṛttayaḥ (f. nom. pl.) fluctuations (see I.2)
pañcatayaḥ (m. nom. sg.) fivefold, having five parts; from pañca (five)
kliṣṭa (m.) afflicted, painful, troubling; from √*kliś* (torment, distress)
akliṣṭāḥ (m. or f. nom. pl.) not afflicted, untroubled, undisturbed; a (not) + *kliṣṭa* (see above) [end of DV cpd.]

The fluctuations are fivefold: afflicted or nonafflicted

6. *pramāṇa-viparyaya-vikalpa-nidrā-smṛtayaḥ*
pramāṇa (n.) valid cognition, correct notion, right perception; *pra* (before, forward) + *māna* (means of proof, demonstrating) from √*mā* (measure, prepare, display)
viparyaya (m.) misconception, error, misapprehension; *vi* (asunder, away) + *pari* (around) + *aya*, from √*i* (go, flow, get about)
vikalpa (m.) conceptualization, imagination; *vi* (asunder, away) + *kalpa*, from √*klp* (correspond, in accordance with, suitable to)
nidrā (f.) sleep, slumber; *ni* (down, into) + √*drā* (sleep)
smṛtayaḥ (m. nom. pl.) memory; from √*smṛ* (remember) [end DV cpd.]

Valid cognition, error, conceptualization, sleep, and memory.

7. *pratyakṣa-anumāna-āgamāḥ pramāṇāni*

pratyakṣa (m.) direct perception, apprehension by the senses; *prati* (against, back) + *akṣa* (organ of sense, eye), from √ *akṣ* (reach, penetrate, embrace)

anumāna (m.) inference, consideration, reflection; *anu* (along, after) + *māna* (means of proof, demonstration, from √ *mā* (measure, prepare, display)

āgamāḥ (m. nom. pl.) a traditional doctrine or precept, a sacred work; *ā* (hither, unto) + *gama* (going), from √ *gam* (go, more) [end of DV cpd.]

pramāṇāni (n. nom. pl.) valid cognitions (see I.6)

Valid cognitions are perception, inference, and valid testimony.

8. *viparyayo mithyā-jñānam atad rūpa-pratiṣṭham*

viparyayah (m.) error (see I.6)

mithyā (ind.) false, untrue, incorrect; from √ *mith* (altercate, dispute angrily)

jñānam (n. nom. sg.) knowledge, understanding; from √ *jñā* (know, be acquainted with)

atad (n. nom. sg. pronoun) not that

rūpa (n.) form, outward appearance, shape (see I.3)

pratiṣṭham (n. nom. sg.) resting place, base, foundation; *prati* (against, back) + *sthā* (stand, take a position) [end of TP7 cpd.]

Error is false knowledge, without foundation in form.

9. *śabda-jñānānupātī vastu-śūnyo vikalpaḥ*

śabda (m.) word, sound, voice, tone, speech

jñāna (n.) knowledge (see I.8)

anupātī (m. nom. sg.) following as a consequence or result; *anu* (along, after) + *pātin* (falling, rising, appearing), from √ *pat* (fly, fall) [end of TP3 cpd.]

vastu (n.) thing, object, article; from √ *vas* (live, dwell, remain, abide)

śūnyaḥ (m. nom. sg.) empty, void, possessing nothing; from

√ *śū, śvā, śvi* (swell) [end of TP6 cpd.]
vikalpaḥ (m. nom. sg.) conceptualization (see I.6)

Conceptualization is the result of words and ideas empty of object.

10. *abhāva-pratyaya-ālambanā vṛttir nidrā*
abhāva (m.) non-becoming, not appearing; *a* (not) + *bhāva* (becoming, being, existing); from √ *bhū* (be, become, exist)
pratyaya (m.) intention,firm conviction, basis; *prati* (against, back) + *aya* (going), from √ *i* (go) [first part of cpd.; TP6]
ālambanā (f. nom. sg.) based or depending on, supporting; *ā* (hither, unto) + *lambana* (hanging down), from √ *lamb* (hang down) [end of cpd.; TP7]
vṛttiḥ (f. nom. sg.) fluctuation (see I.2)
nidrā sleep (see I.6)

The sleep fluctuation is based on the intention of nonbecoming.

11. *anubhūta-viṣaya-asaṃpramoṣaḥ smṛtiḥ*
anubhūta (m.) experienced, perceived, understood; *anu* (along, after) + *bhūta* (become, existing, present), from √ *bhū* (be, become, exist)
viṣaya (m.) condition, dominion, sphere of activity or concern, an object of sense; probably from √ *viṣ* (be active) or *vi* (asunder, away) + √ *si* (extend) [first part of cpd., KD]
asaṃpramoṣaḥ (m. nom. sg.) recollection, not letting drop or be set free; *a* (not) + *sam* (together) + *pra* (before, forward) + *moṣa* (robbery, theft, stealing), from √ *muṣ* (steal) [end of cpd.; TP6]
smṛtiḥ (f. nom. sg.) memory (see I.6)

Memory is the recollection of an experienced condition.

12. *abhyāsa-vairāgyābhyāṃ tan nirodhaḥ*
abhyāsa (m.) practice, repeated exercise, discipline, study; *abhi*

(to, unto, toward) + *āsa* (seat), from √ *ās* (sit quietly)

vairāgyābhyām (n. instr. du.) dispassion, freedom from worldly desires; from *virāga, vi* (asunder, away) + *rāga* (passion, love, desire), from √ *rañj* (be reddened, be attracted) [end of DV cpd.]

tad (ind.) there, in that place

nirodhaḥ (m. nom. sg.) restraint, control, suppression (see I.2)

Through practice and dispassion arises restraint.

13. *tatra sthitau yatno'bhyāsaḥ*

tatra (ind.) there

sthitau (f. loc. sg.) remaining in a state, continued existence, steadiness; from √ *sthā* (stand)

yatnaḥ (m. nom. sg.) effort, activity of will, zeal; from √ *yat* (place in order)

abhyāsaḥ (m. nom. sg.) practice (see I.12)

Effort in remaining there is practice.

14. *sa tu dīrgha-kāla-nairantarya-satkāra-āsevito dṛḍha-bhūmiḥ*

saḥ (m. nom. sg. pron.) it, this, that

tu (ind.) but, now, then

dīrgha (adj.) long

kāla (m.) time; from √ *kal* (drive, produce) [first part of cpd., KD]

nairantarya (n.) uninterruptedness, continuousness; *nair (vṛddhi* form of *nir*, out, away from) + *antarya*, from *antara* (interior, near, intimate) [second part of TP3 cpd.]

sat kāra (m.) care, attention, consideration; from *sat* (being), from √ *as* (is); + *kāra* (making, doing, working), from √ *kṛ* (do, make, perform) [third part of cpd., TP3]

āsevitaḥ (m. nom. sg.) frequented, practiced assiduously; *ā* (hither, unto) + *sevita* (dwelt in, visited, frequented), from √ *sev* (stay, dwell) [end of cpd., KD] *dṛḍha* (m.) fixed, firm, hard, strong; p.p.p. from √ *dṛṃh* (be firm or strong)

bhūmiḥ (f. nom. sg.) situation, place, earth; from √ *bhū* (be, exist) [end of KD cpd.]

But that is firmly situated when carefully attended to for a long time without interruption.

15. *dṛṣṭa-anuśravika-viṣaya-vitṛṣṇasya vaśīkāra-saṃjñā vairāgyam*

dṛṣṭa (m.) seen, observed, perceived; p.p.p. from *dṛś* (see, apprehend)

anuśravika (m.) according to hearing, based on tradition; from *anu* (along, after) + *śravika*, from √ *śru* (hear) [first part of cpd., DV]

viṣaya (m.) condition, object of sense (see I.11) [second part of cpd., KD]

vitṛṣṇasya (m. gen. sg.) of one free from thirst, desirelessness; *vi* (asunder, away) + *tṛṣ* (be thirsty or desirous) [end of TP4 cpd.]

vaśīkāra (m.) mastery, subjugating, bringing into subjection; *vaśī* (will, desire), from √ *vaś* (command, desire) + *kāra* (making), from √ *kṛ* (do, act)

saṃjñā (f. nom. sg.) knowledge, clear conception; *s* (together) + *jñā* (know, understand) [end of TP6 cpd.]

vairāgyam (n. nom. sg.) dispassion (see I.12)

Dispassion is the knowledge of mastery in one who thirsts not for conditions seen or heard.

16. *tat paraṃ puruṣa-khyāter guṇa-vaitṛṣṇyam*

tad (n. nom. sg. pron.) that, this

param (n. nom. sg.) highest, best, supreme; from √ *pṛ* (surpass, excel)

puruṣa (m.) man, human, primeval man as source of everything, highest self; sometimes translated as soul or spirit; in Sāṃkhya, defined as inactive witness; probably from *pṛī* (fill, make complete)

khyāteḥ (f. abl. sg.) from discernment, perception, knowledge; from *khyā* (see, make known, proclaim) [end of TP6 cpd.]

guṇa (m.) thread or strand; quality, attribute; in Sāṃkhya, the three *guṇas (sattva,* lightness; *rajas,* activity; *tamas,* darkness) constitute *Prakṛti* and hence all created things

vaitṛṣṇyam (n. nom. sg.) freedom from desire; strengthened form of *vitṛṣṇa* (see I.15) [end of TP4 cpd.]

That highest (dispassion) - thirstlessness for the *guṇas* - [proceeds] from the discernment of *puruṣa*.

17. *vitarka-vicāra-ānanda-asmitā-anugamāt-saṃprajñ ātaḥ*

vitarka (m.) discursive thought, deliberation, consideration, doubt; conjecture, supposition; from *vi* (asunder, away) + *tarka* (conjecture, speculation), from √*tark* (conjecture, reason, reflect)

vicāra (m.) mode of proceeding; reflection; "clear vision" (Bengali Baba), from *vi* (asunder, away) + *cāra* (going, motion), from √*car* (go, move)

ānanda (m.) bliss, happiness, enjoyment; from *ā* (hither, unto) + *nanda* (joy, delight), from √*nand* (rejoice, be glad)

asmitā (f.) I-am-ness, egotism; from *asmi* first person singular indicative of *as* (be) + *tā*, feminine suffix denoting "having the quality of" [end of series of DV cpds.]

anugamāt (m. abl. sg.) following, going after; association; from *anu* (along, after) + *gama* (going), from √*gam* (go) [end of TP3 cpd.]

saṃprajñ ātaḥ (m. nom. sg.) with consciousness, cognitive; distinguished, discerned, known accurately; *sam* (together) + *pra* (before, forward) + *jñ āta* (known, understood, perceived), from √*jñ ā* (know)

Saṃprajñāta **[arises] from association with discursive throught, reflection, bliss, and I-am-ness.**

18. *virāma-pratyaya-abhyāsa-pūrvaḥ saṃskāra-śeṣo'nyaḥ*
virāma (m.) cessation, termination, end; *vi* (asunder, away) + *rāma*, from √*ram* (stop, set at rest)
pratyaya (m.) intention (see I.10) [end of TP6 cpd.]
abhyāsa (m.) practice (see I.12) [end of DV cpd.]
pūrvaḥ (m. nom. sg.) former, prior, preceding [end of TP3 cpd.]
saṃskāra (m.) impression left by action done in the past which conditions future actions; "subliminal activator" (Feuerstein); "habitual potency" (Baba); latency; from *sam* (together) + *kāra* (doing), from √*kṛ* (do)
śeṣaḥ (m. nom. sg.) remainder, residue; here translated as only; from √*śiṣ* (leave, leave remaining) [end of BV cpd.]
anyaḥ (m. nom. sg.) other, different

The other (state)* has *saṃskāra* only and is preceded by practice and the intention of cessation.
*Referred to by Vyāsa as "*asaṃprajñāta samādhi.*"

19. *bhava-pratyayo videha-prakṛti-layānām*
bhava (m.) becoming, coming into existence; from √*bhū* (be, exist)
pratyayaḥ (m. nom. sg.) intention, (see I.10) [end of TP6 cpd.]
videha (m.) discarnate, bodiless, incorporeal; *vi* (asunder, away) + *deha* (body), from √*dih* (smear, annoint) [first part of DV cpd.]
prakṛti (f.) creative, active aspect of reality, as opposed to *puruṣa*; sometimes translated as nature or primary matter; composed of and inseparable from the three *guṇas* (see I.16); from *pra* (before, forward) + *kṛti* (act of doing or creating), from √*kṛ* (do, make)

layānām (m. gen. pl.) absorption in, melting; clinging to; from √ *lī* (melt, cling) [end of BV cpd.]

Of the ones who are absorbed in *prakṛti* and discarnate, [there is] an intention of becoming.
(These are deemed mild (see I.22).)

20. *śraddhā-vīrya-smṛti-samādhi-prajñā-pūrvaka itareṣām*
śraddhā (f.) faith, confidence, trust
vīrya (n.) energy, strength, power, from *vīra* (brave or eminent man, hero)
smṛti (f.) mindfulness (see I.6)
samādhi (m.) absorption, concentration, putting together, completion, intense absorption; from *sam* (together) + *ā* (hither, unto) + *dhi*, from √ *dhā* (put, place)
prajñā (f.) wisdom, knowledge, insight; from *pra* (before, forward) + √ *jñā* (know, understand) [end of series of DV cpds.]
pūrvakaḥ (m. nom. sg.) preceded or accompanied by; from *pūrva* (see I.18) + *ka*, suffix indicating possession [end of TP3 cpd.]
itareṣām (m. gen. pl.) of the others

Of the others it is preceded by faith, energy, mindfulness, *samādhi*, and wisdom.
(These may be seen as medium.)

21. *tīvra-saṃvegānām āsannaḥ*
tīvra (m.) strong, intense, acute
saṃvegānām (m. gen. pl.) of the intense or vehement ones; *sam* (together) + *vega* (impetuosity, excitement), from √ *vij* (be agitated, tremble) [end of KD cpd.]; related to Pali word for "shock" or "thrill"
āsannaḥ (m. nom. sg.) near, proximate; from *ā* (hither, unto) + *sanna* (set down), from *sad* (sit)

The strongly intense ones are near.
(These may be seen as ardent.)

22. *mṛdu-madhya-adhimātratvāt tato'pi viśeṣaḥ*

mṛdu (m.) mild, soft, weak; from √ *mṛd* (trample down)
madhya (m.) moderate, standing between two, middle
adhimātratvāt (m. abl. sg.) above measure, more than usual, ardent; *adhi* (over, on) + *mātra* (measure, quantity), from √ *mā* (measure) + *tva*, suffix meaning "having the quality of"
tatah (ind.) hence, from that
api (ind.) also, indeed, very
viśeṣaḥ (m. nom. sg.) distinction, difference, peculiarity; *vi* (asunder, away) + *śeṣa* (remainder), from √ *śiṣ (leave)*

Hence the distinctions of mild, moderate, and ardent.

23. *Īśvara-praṇidhānād vā*

Īśvara (m.) master, lord, king; able to do, capable; from √ *īś* (command, rule) + *vara* (valuable, eminent, choicest), from √ *vṛ* (choose)
praṇidhānāt (m. abl. sg.) dedication, attention paid to, respectful conduct; *pra* (before, forward) + *ni* (down, into) + *dhāna* (containing, holding), from √ *dhā* (put, place) [end of TP7 cpd.]
vā (ind.) or

Or from dedication to *Īśvara*.

24. *kleśa-karma-vipākāśayair aparāmṛṣṭaḥ puraṣa-viśeṣa īsvaraḥ*

kleśa (m.) affliction, pain, distress ; from √ *kliś* (trouble, afflict)
karma (n.) action, work; from √ *kṛ* (co, make)
vipāka (m.) fruition, ripening; effect, result; *vi* (away) + *pāka* (cooking), from √ *pac* (cook)

āśayair (m. instr. pl.) residue, stock, balance of fruits from past actions; *ā* (hither, unto) + *śaya* (lying, resting, abiding), from √ *śī* (rest, lie) [end of DV cpd.]

aparāmṛṣṭaḥ (m. nom. sg.) untouched; *a* (not) + *parā* (away, off, aside) + *mṛṣṭa* (touched), from √ *mṛś* (touch, feel)

puruṣa (m.) (see I.16)

viśeṣaḥ (m. nom. sg.) distinct (see I.22) [end of TP6]

īśvaraḥ (m. nom. sg.) (see I.23)

Īśvara is a distinct *puruṣa* untouched by afflictions, actions, fruitions, or their residue.

25. *tatra niratiśayaṃ sarva-jña-bījam*

tatra (ind.) there

niratiśyaṃ (n. nom. sg.) unsurpassed, unexcelled; *nir* (out, away from) + *ati* (over, beyond, past) + *śaya* (lying, resting), from √ *śi* (rest, lie)

sarva (n.) all, every, whole, entire

jña (m.) knowing, knowledge; from √ *jñā* (know, understand) [end of KD cpd.]

bījam (n. nom. sg.) seed, germ, origin [end of TP6 cpd.]

There the seed of omniscience is unsurpassed.

26. *pūrveṣām api guruḥ kālena anavacchedāt*

pūrveṣām (m. gen. pl.) of the prior ones; see I.18

api (ind.) also, even

guruḥ (m. nom. sg.) teacher, venerable person, preceptor

kālena (m. instr. sg.) by time; from √ *kal* (drive forward, produce)

anavacchedāt (m. abl. sg.) from not being cut, or limited or separated; from *an* (not) + *ava* (down, from, away) + *cheda* (cutting off, interrupting) from √ *chid* (cut, amputate)

Due to its being unlimited by time, it is the teacher of the

prior ones.

27. *tasya vācakaḥ praṇavaḥ*
tasya (m. gen. sg.) its
vācakaḥ (m. nom. sg.) expression; from √ *vac* (speak)
praṇavaḥ (m. nom. sg.) the sacred syllable *"OM"*; from *pra* (before, forward) + *nava*, from √ *nu* (sound, shout, exult)

Its expression is *praṇava (OM)*.

28. *taj japas tad artha-bhāvanam*
tat (n. nom. sg. pron.) that
japas (m. nom. sg.) repetition, repeating in a low voice; from √ *jap* (whisper, mutter)
tad (n. nom. sg. pron.) that
artha (m. or n.) meaning, aim, purpose
bhāvanam (n. nom. sg.) realization, causing to be, effecting, manifesting; from causative form of √ *bhū* (be, exist) [end of TP6 cpd.]

Repetition of it and realization of its purpose [should be made].

29. *tataḥ pratyak-cetanā-adhigamo'py-antarāya-abhāvaś-ca*
tataḥ (ind.) thence, from it
pratyak (m.) combining form of *pratyañc*, inward, in opposite direction
cetanā (f.) consciousness, understanding, sense; from √ *cit* (perceive, know, appear) [end of KD cpd.]
adhigamo (m. nom. sg.) attainment, mastery, acquirement; *adhi* (over, on) + *gama* (going), from √ *gam* (go) [end of TP6 cpd.]
api (ind.) also, even
antarāya (m.) obstacle, intervention; *antar* (between) + *āya*, from √ *i* (go)

abhāvaḥ (m. nom. sg.) non-arising, disappearance, absence; *a* (not) + *bhāva* (being), from √ *bhu* (be, exist)

Thus inward consciousness is attained and obstacles do not arise.

30. *vyādhi-styāna-saṃśaya-pramāda-ālasya-avirati-bhrānti-darśana-alabdha-bhūmikatva-anavasthitatvāni citta-vikṣepās te'ntarāyāḥ*

vyādhi (m.) sickness, disorder, ailment; *vi* (asunder, away) + *ā* (hither, unto) + *dhi*, from √ dhā (put, place)

styāna (m.) dullness, thickness, rigidity; from √ *styā* (stiffen)

saṃśaya (m.) doubt, hesitation, uncertainty; *sam* (together) + *śaya* (lying, sleeping), from √ *śī* (rest, lie)

pramāda (m.) carelessness, negligence; intoxication, madness; *pra* (before, forward) + *māda* (drunkenness), from √ *mad* (be intoxicated, revel or delight in)

ālasya (n.) laziness, idleness, sloth; derived from

alasa, *a* (not) + *lasa* (lively, shining, moving about), from √ *las* (shine, flash; play, frolic)

avirati (f.) sense indulgence, intemperance; sensuality (Baba); worldliness (Woods); lack of detachment (Rukmani); *a* (not) + *vi* (asunder, away) + *rati* (pleasure, enjoyment) from √ *ram* (delight, enjoy carnally) [end of series DV cpds.]

bhrānti (f.) false, confusing, erroneous; from √ *bhram* (wander about, waver)

darśana (m.) view, observation, understanding; from √ *dṛś* (see, perceive) [end of KD cpd.]

alabdha (m.) unobtained, not having attained; *a* (not) + *labdha*, p.p.p. from √ *labh* (obtain, take)

bhūmikatva (n.) stage, place, step; from *bhūmi* (earth, position, stage) + *ka* (suffix meaning "having") + *tva* (suffix meaning "quality") [end of KD cpd.]

anavasthitatvāni (n. nom. pl.) instability, unsteadiness; from *an* (not) + *ava* (down, from, away) + *sthita* (standing, established), from √ *sthā* (stand) + *tva* (suffix meaning quality) [end of DV cpds.]

citta (n.) consciousness (see I.2)

vikṣepāḥ (m. nom. pl.) distraction, scattering, dispersion; *vi* (away, asunder) + *kṣepa* (throwing, casting), from √ *kṣip* (throw, send) [end of TP6 cpd.]

te (m. nom. pl.) these

antarāyāḥ (m. nom. pl.) obstacles (see I.29)

These obstacles, distractions of the mind, are: sickness, dullness, doubt, carelessness, laziness, sense addiction, false view, non-attainment of a stage, and instability.

31. *duḥkha-daurmanasya-aṅgam ejayatva-śvāsa-praśvāsā vikṣe-pa-sahabhuvaḥ*

duḥkha (n.) dissatisfaction, pain, uneasiness, sorrow, trouble, difficulty; from √ *duṣ* (difficult, wicked, bad, inferior) + *kha* (axle hole, cavity, hollow, cave)

daurmanasya (n.) despair, depression, dejectedness; *daur* (strengthened form of √ *duṣ* (see above) + *manasya* (have in mind, think), from √ *man* (think, conjecture) [end of DV cpd.]

aṅgam (n. nom. sg.) body, limb, member [end of KD cpd.]

ejayatva (m.) unsteadiness, trembling, shaking; causative derivative of √ *ej* (stir, move, tremble)
+ *tva* suffix, indicating quality
[Note: Vyāsa links this word with *aṅgam*, though gram matically it is part of a karmadharya compound describing *śvāsa* and *praśvāsa*.]

śvāsa (m.) inhalation, breathing; from √ *śvas* (breathe, respire)

praśvāḥ (m. nom. pl.) breathing out, exhaling; *pra* (before, forward) + *śvāsa* (see above) *vikṣepa (m.) distraction (see I.30)*

sahabhuvaḥ (m. nom. sg.) appearing together, counterpart of; *saha* (together with) + *bhuva*, from √ *bhū* (be, exist) [end of TP6 cpd.]

A dissatisfied, despairing body and unsteady inhalation and exhalation accompany the distractions.

32. *tat pratiṣedha-artham eka-tattva-abhyāsaḥ*

tat (usually n. nom. sg.; here, ind.) it, that; these, them
pratiṣedha (m.) counteracting, preventing, keeping back; *prati* (against, back) + *sedha*, driving away, from √ *sidh* (repel)
artham (n. nom. sg.) purpose (see I.28)
eka (m.) one; alone, solitary, single
tattva (n.) thing; literally "that-ness," sometimes translated as principle, essence; elementary property; "entity" (Woods, Rukmani)
abhyāsaḥ (m. nom. sg.) practice (see I.12)

For the purpose of counteracting them, [there is] the practice of one thing *(eka-tattva)*.

Various practices are listed below.

33. *maitrī-karuṇā-muditā-upekṣāṇāṃ sukha-duḥkha-puṇya-apuṇya-viṣayāṇāṃ bhāvanātaś citta prasādanam*

maitrī (f.) friendliness, good will, benevolence
karuṇā (f.) compassion, pity; from √ *kṛ* (do, make) or √ *kṛ* (pour out, scatter)
muditā (f.) happiness, gladness, joy; from √ *mud* (be happy, rejoice)
upekṣāṇāṃ (f. gen. pl.) equanimity, indifference; literally, overlooking; *upa* (to, unto) + *īkṣa* from √ *īkṣ* (see, look) [end of DV cpds.]
sukha (n.) pleasure, happiness, comfort, ease, virtue; *su* (good) + *kha* (axle-hole)
duḥkha (n.) dissatisfaction, pain (see I.31)
puṇya (n.) merit, virtue, righteousness, goodness, auspicious, propitious; from √ *puṇ* (act virtuously) or √ *puṣ* (thrive, cause to prosper)

apuṇya (n.) absence of merit, evil, non-virtuous; from *a* (not) + √ *puṇ* or √ *puṣ* (see above) [end of DV cpd.]
viṣayāṇāṃ (m. gen. pl.) of conditions, spheres of activity (see I.11) [end of TP6 cpd.; genitive absolute construction]
bhāvanātaś (ind.) from cultivation; producing, effecting, projecting; *bhāvanā* (f.) causative from of √ *bhū* (be, exist) + *tas*, indeclinable ablative suffix meaning "from"
citta (n.) consciousness, mind (see I.2)
prasādanam (n. nom. sg.) clarification, calmness, tranquility, clearness; *pra* (before, forward) + *sādana* (causing to settle down), from √ *sad* (sit) [end of TP6 cpd.]

Clarification of the mind [results] from the cultivation of friendliness, compassion, happiness, and equanimity in conditions of pleasure, dissatisfaction, merit, and absence of merit, respectively.

34. *pracchardana-vidhāraṇābhyāṃ vā prāṇasya*
pracchardana (n.) expulsion, exhalation, emitting; from *pra* (before, forward) + *cchardana*, from √ *chṛd* (spew, eject)
vidhāraṇābhyāṃ(m. instr. du.) of the retention, holding, checking; from *vi* (asunder, away) + *dhārana* (holding, bearing, keeping), from √ *dhṛ* (hold, keep)
prāṇasya (m. gen. sg.) of breath; life; *pra* (before, forward) + *ana* (breath, respiration), from √ *an* (breathe)

Or by expulsion and retention of breath.

35. *viṣaya-vatī vā pravṛttir utpannā manasaḥ sthiti-nibandanī*
viṣayavatī (f. nom. sg.) having a condition; involved in a sphere of sense activity; taking up an object of desire; *viṣaya* (see I.11 and I.23) + *vatī*, feminine form of suffix indicating possessive adjective
vā (ind.) or

pravṛttir (f. nom. sg.) activity, moving onward, "cognition" in regard to *Y.S.* according to Monier-Williams; *pra* (before, forward) + *vṛtti* (see I.2), from √ *vṛt* (turn, revolve, move)

utpannā (f. nom. sg.) risen, born, produced; *ut* (up, forth) + *pannā* (fallen, gone), from √ *pad* (fall)

manasaḥ (n. gen. sg.) of the mind, organ of perception and cognition; from √ *man* (think, believe, conjecture)

sthiti (f.) steadiness, standing upright, staying; from √ *sthā* (stand, take up a position)

nibandhanī (m. nom. sg.) holding, binding; causing; *ni* (down, into) + *bandha*, from √ *bandh* (bind) + *in* (possessive suffix) [end of BV cpd.]

Or steady binding of the mind-organ arises in the activity of involvement with a condition.

[Vyāsa gives examples of directly perceived sensations as stabilizers of the mind.]

36. *viśokā vā jyotiṣmatī* .

viśokā (f. nom. sg.) sorrowless, without pain or afflication; *vi* (away, asunder) + *śoka* (sorrow, affliction, anquish, trouble), from √ *śuc* (suffer violent heat or pain; be afflicted)

vā (ind.) or

jyotiṣmatī (f. nom. sg.) having illumination, light, brightness; *jyotis*, from √ *jyut* (shine upon, illuminate) + *matī*, feminine form of suffix indicating possessive adjective.

Or having sorrowless illumination.

37. *vīta-rāga-viṣayaṃ vā cittam*

vīta (m.) free; released, gone away, departed, disappeared; *vi* (asunder, away) + *ita*, from √ *i* (go)

rāga (m.) attachment, passion, love, desire; from √ *rañj* (be

reddened, be attracted) (see I.12) [end of KD cpd.]
viṣayaṃ (n. nom. sg.) condition (see I.11)
√ *a* (ind.) or
cittam (n. nom. sg.) consciousness (see I.2)

Or [on a] mind in a condition free from attachment.

38. *svapna-nidrā-jñ āna-ālambanaṃ vā*
svapna (m.) dream, sleep; from √ *svap* (sleep)
nidrā (f.) sleep, sleepiness; *ni* (down, into) + √ *drā* (sleep) [end of DV cpd.]
jñ āna (n.) knowledge (see I.8) [end of TP5 epd.]
ālambanaṃ (n. nom. sg.) resting or depending on, hanging from; *ā* (hither, unto) + *lambana* (hanging down), from √ *laṃb* (hang, dangle, sink) [end of TP7 cpd.]
vā (ind.) or

Or resting on knowledge [derived] from dream or sleep.

39. *yathā abhimata-dhyānād-vā*
yathā (ind.) as
abhimata (m.) desired, longed for, wished; *abhi* (to, toward), + *mata* (thought, sentiment), from √ *man* (think, believe, conjecture)
dhyānād (m. abl. sg.) from meditation or contemplation; derived from √ *dhyai* (meditate, think of, contemplate) [end of KD cpd.]
vā (ind.) or

Or from meditation as desired.

40. *parama-aṇu-parama-mahattva-anto'sya vaśīkāraḥ*
parama (m.) most; extreme limit; superlative form of *para* (more or better), derived from √ *pṛ* (surpass)
aṇu (m.) small, fine, minute [end of KD cpd.]

parama (m.) most (see above)
mahattva (n.) greatness, great size or extent, magnitude; *maha* (great, mighty, strong), from √ *mah* (magnify) + *tva* (suffix indicating "-ness" or essence) [end of KD cpd.]
antaḥ (m. nom. sg.) end, conclusion; indicates from ... to [end of TP6 cpd.]
asya (m. gen. sg. pron.) his, of him
vaśīkāraḥ (m. nom. sg.) mastery (see I.15)

Mastery of it [extends] from the smallest to the greatest.

41. *kṣīṇa-vṛtter abhijātasya-iva maṇer grahītṛ-grahaṇa-grāhyeṣu tat-stha-tad-añjanatā samāpattiḥ*

kṣīṇa (m.) diminished, expended, worn away, waning; from √*kṣi (destroy, make an end to)*
vṛttes (f. gen. sg.) fluctuation (see 1.1) [end of BV cpd.]
abhijātasya (m. gen. sg.) precious, noble, handsome, well-born; *abhi* (to, toward) + *jāta* (born), from √*jan* (be born)
iva (ind.) like
maṇes (m. gen. sg.) of a jewel, gem
grahītṛ (m.) grasper, taker, experiencer; from √*grabh* (grab, seizer) + *tṛ*, suffix indicating agency
grahaṇa (m.) grasping, seizing, holding, act of experiencing, from √*grabh* (see above)
grahyeṣu (m. loc. pl.) in the grasped (lit., to be grasped, seized, or taken); that which is experienced, gerundive derived from √*grabh* (see above) [end of DV cpd.]
tat (ind.) that, it
stha (m.) standing, staying, abiding; from √*sthā* (stand, remain)
tad (ind.) that, it
añjanatā (f. nom. sg.) made clear, annointed, caused to appear; *añjana*, from √*añj* (annoint) + (*tā*, feminine suffix indicating quality
[tat-stha-tad-añjana-tā, literally "there standing, there

annointed-ness" is translated by Monier Williams as "asuming the color of any near object"]

samāpattiḥ (f. nom. sg.) unity, coming together;

sam (together) + *ā* (hither, unto) + *patti*, from $\sqrt{pat}$ (fall, fly)

[The accomplished mind] of diminished fluctuations, like a precious (or clear) jewel assuming the color of any near object, has unity among grasper, grasping, and grasped.

This translation is at variance with Vyāsas intpretation, which renders the *Sūtra* "the [mind] of diminished fluctuations like a clear jewel assuming the color of grasper, grasping, or grasped (seqentially) has unity." Vyāsa posits three types of unity; we posit one form of unity where in all three aspects of grasping etc., collapse, regardless of what is grasped, gross or subtle.

42. *tatra śabda-artha-jñāna-vikalpaiḥ saṃkīrṇā savitarkā samā pattiḥ*

tatra (ind.) there, in that

śabda (m.) word (see I.9)

artha (m. or n.) purpose (see I.28)

jñāna (n.) knowledge (see I.8) [end of DV cpd.]

vikalpaiḥ (m.instr. pl.) conceptualization (see I.6) [end of TP6 cpd.]

saṃkīrṇā (f. nom. sg.) commingling, mixed, interspersed; confusion; *sam* (together) + kīrṇa (scattered, thrown), from $\sqrt{kṛ}$ (scatter)

savitarkā (f. nom. sg.) with thought, cognition, or deliberation; *sa* (with) + *vi* (asunder, away) + *tarka* (conjecture, reasoning)

samāpattiḥ (f. nom. sg.) unity (see I.41)

***Savitarkā* unity is the commingling by conceptualization of word, purpose, and knowledge.**

43. *smṛti-pariśuddhau sva rūpa-śūnyā-iva-artha-mātra-nirbhāsā nirvitarkā*

smṛti (f.) memory (see I.6)

pariśuddhau (m. loc. sg.) purified, clean; *pari* (around) + *śuddhi*, from *śudh* (purify, cleanse) [end of TP6 cpd.]

sva rūpa (n.)own-form (see I.3)

śūnyā (f. nom. sg.) empty (see I.9) [end of TP6 cpd.]

iva (ind.) like, as if

artha (m. or n.) purpose; meaning (see I.28)

mātra (m.) only, nothing but, entirely; also means measure, quantity, element; from *mā* (measure) [end of TP6 cpd.]

nirbhāsā (f. nom. sg.) shines forth, is apparent or illumined; *nir* (assunder, away) + *bhāsa* (light, lustre, brightness), from *bhās* (illuminate, shine) [end of KD cpd.]

nirvitarkā (f. nom. sg.) beyond thought or cognition; *nir* (out, away from) + *vi* (asunder, away) + *tarka* (conjecture, reasoning)

***Nirvitarkā* is when memory is purified, as if emptied of its own form, and the purpose alone shines forth.**

When the memory is purified, the superimposition of karmic deposits is halted and the purpose, in this case the object of perceptions, is not finged with the past. See III. 3..

44. *etayaiva savicārā nirvicārā ca sūkṣma-viṣayā vyākhyātā*

etayā (f. instr. sg.) by this

eva (ind.) thus

savicārā (f. nom. sg.) with reflection, consideration; *sa* (with) + *vi* (asunder, away) + *cāra* (going, motion, progression), from √*car* (go, wander)

nirvicāra (f. nom. sg.) beyond reflection or consideration; *nir* (asunder, away) + *vicāra* (see above)

ca (ind.) and

sūkṣma (m.) subtle, fine, thin; probably related to √*siv*(sew)

viṣayā (f. nom. sg.) condition (see I.11) [end of BV cpd.]

vyākhyātā (f. nom. sg.) explained, fully detailed; *vi* (asunder, away) + *ā* (unto) + *khyātā* (named, known), from √*khyā* (name, declare)

Similarly explained are *savicāra* and *nirvicāra* which are subtle conditions.

The levels of unity *(samāpatti)* are explained as four fold! *savitarka* (with gross object); *nirvitarka* (free of gross object); *savicāra* (with subtle object); *nirvicāra* (free of subtle object).

45. *sūkṣma-viṣayatvaṃ ca aliṅga-paryavasānam*

sūkṣma (m.) subtle (see I.44)

viṣayatvaṃ (n. nom. sg.) condition; nature of condition; *viṣaya* (see I.11) + *tva*, suffix indicating ness or nature of [end of KD cpd.]

ca (ind.) and

aliṅga (n.) undesignated, bearing no marks, undifferentiated, unmanifest; said by vyāsa to refer to *prakṛti*, the most subtle cause; *a* (not) + *liṅga* (sign, mark), from √*liṅg* (paint, change) *paryavasānam (n. nom. sg.)* termination, end, conclusion; *pari* (around) + *ava* (down) + *sāna*, from √*sā* (bind) [end of TP7 cpd.]

And the subtle condition terminates in the undesignated.

46. *tā eva sabījaḥ samādhiḥ*

tāḥ (f. nom. pl.) these

eva (ind.) indeed

sabījah (m. nom. sg.) with seed or source; *sa* (with) + *bīja* (seed, germ, primary cause)

samādhiḥ (m. nom. sg.) concentration (see I.20)

These are *samādhi* with seed.

47. *nirvicāra-vaiśāradye' dhyātma-prasādaḥ*

nirvicāra (m.) beyond reflection (see I.44)

vaiśāradye (n. loc. sg.) skill in, expertness, clearness of intellect; strengthened form of *viśārada* (experienced, skilled), *VI* (a way) + *śārada* (autumn) [end of TP3 cpd.]

adhyātma (n.) authentic self, inner-being; *adhi* (over, on) + *ātma* (self, sometimes translated as soul), from √*an* (breathe) or √*at* (move)

prasādaḥ (m. nom. sg.) clarity, brightness, purity (see I.33)

In skill with *nirvicāra*, clarity of authentic self arises.

48. *ṛtaṃ bharā tatra prajñā*

ṛtaṃ (n. nom. sg.) truth, righteousness, *dharma*, order, norm; refers to the order established by sacrifice or the movement of life, from √*ṛ* (go towards, obtain, reach)

bharā (f. nom. sg.) bearing, carrying; from √*bhṛ (bear)*

tatra (adv.) there

prajñā (f. nom. sg.) wisdom, knowledge, intelligence; from *pra* (before, forward) + √*jña* (know)

There the wisdom is *ṛtaṃ* - bearing.

This wisdom sustains the movement of life. Ignorance is to fall from this order.

49. *śruta-anumāna-prajñābhyām anya-viṣayā viśeṣa-arthatvāt*

śruta (m.) tradition, that which is heard; from √*śru* (hear)

anumāna (m.) inference (see I.7) [end of DV cpd.]

prajñābhyām (f. abl. du.) from wisdom (see I.48) [end of TP5 cpd.]

anya (m.) different, other

viṣayā (f. nom. sg.) condition (see I.11) [end of KD cpd.; agrees with *prajñā* of prior *sūtra*]

viśeṣa (m.) distinct (see I.22)

arthatvāt (m. abl. sg.) due to purpose, because of its aim; from *artha* (see I.28) + *tva*, suffix indicating quality [end of KD cpd.]

Its condition is different from heard or inferred knowledge because of its distinct purpose.

As in I.43, the purpose is to enable the perception of *puraṣa.*

50. *taj-jaḥ saṃskāro'nya-saṃskāra-pratibandhī*

taj (n.) that

jaḥ (m. nom. sg.) born, arisen, sprung; from $\sqrt{jan}$ (generate, produce) [end of TP5 cpd.]

saṃskārah (m. nom. sg.) (see I.18)

anya (m.) other

saṃskāra (m.) (see I.18) [end of KD cpd.]

pratibandhī (m. nom. sg.) obstructing, preventing, impeding; *prati* (against, back) + *bandhin*, from $\sqrt{bandh}$ (bind) + *in*, suffix indicating possession [end of TP2 cpd.]

The *saṃskāra* born of it obstructs other *saṃskāras.*

51. *tasya api nirodhe sarva-nirodhān nirbījaḥ samādhiḥ*

tasya (m. gen. sg.) of it

api (ind.) also, even

nirodhe (m. loc. sg.) in being restricted, suppressed (see I.2)

sarva (m.) all

nirodhāt (m. abl. sg.) from being restricted (see I.2)

nirbījaḥ (m.nom. sg.) without seed; *nir* (away from, out) + *bīja* (see I.46)

samādhiḥ (m. nom. sg.) (see I.20)

With even that restricted, everything is restricted and that is seedless *samādhi*.

II. *Sādhana Pāda*

1. *tapaḥ-svādhyāya-īśvara-praṇidhānāni kriyā-yogaḥ*
   tapaḥ (n.) austerity, self-discipline, creative heat from √*tap* (make hot)
   svādhyāya (m.) self-study; study of sacred texts; *sva* (own) + *adhi* (over, on) + √*a* (hither, unto) + *ya*, from √*i* (go)
   īśvara (m.) (see I.23)
   praṇidhānāni (n. nom.pl.) dedication (see I.23) [end of DV cpd.]
   kriyā (f.) doing, performing, work, action; from √*kṛ* (do, make)
   yogaḥ (m. non. sg.) (see I.1) [end of KD cpd.)

Austerity, self-study, and dedication to *Īśvara* are *kriyā-yoga*.

2. *samādhi-bhāvana-arthaḥ kleśa-tanū-karaṇa-arthaś ca*
   samādhi (m.) (see I:20)
   bhāvana (m.) cultivating, causing to be, manifesting; causative form of √*bhū* (be)
   arthaḥ (m. nom. sg.) purpose (see I:28) [end of TP6 cpd.]
   kleśa (m.) affliction (see I.24)
   tanū (f.) attenuated, lessened, diminished, weakened; from √*tan* (stretch, spin out)
   karaṇa (m.) doing, making, causing effecting; from √*kṛ* (do)
   arthaś (m.) purpose (seeI:28) [end of TP6 cpd.]
   ca (ind.) and

[It is] for the purposes of cultivating *samādhi* and attenuating the afflictions.

3. *avidyā-asmitā-rāga-dveṣa-abhiniveśāh kleśāḥ*
   avidyā (f.) ignorance, nonwisdom, delusion; + *vidyā*, wisdom, from √*vid* (know)
   asmitā (f.) I-am-ness (see I:17)

rāga (m.) attraction (see I:37)

dveṣa (m.) aversion, repulsion, hatred, dislike; from √*dviṣ* (hate)

abhiniveśāḥ (m. nom. pl.) desire for continuity, clinging to life, will to live, tenacity; *abhi* (to, toward) + *ni* (down, into) + *veśa*, from √*viś* (enter) [end of DV cpd.]

kleśāḥ (m. nom. pl.) affliction (see I:24)

Ignorance, I-am-ness, attraction, aversion, and desire for continuity are the afflictions.

4. *avidyā kṣetraṃ uttareṣāṃ prasupta-tanu-vicchina-udārāṇām*

avidyā (f. nom. sg.) ignorance (see II:3)

kṣetraṃ (n. nom. sg.) origin, field, ground; from √*kṣi* (possess)

uttareṣām (m. gen. pl.) of the others

prasupta (m.) dormant, fallen, asleep, inactive, latent; *pra* (before, forward) + *supta*, from √*svap* (sleep)

tanu (m.) attenuated, lessened, diminished; from √*tan* (stretch, spin out)

vicchinna (m.) suppressed, overpowered, interrupted; *vi* (assunder, away) + *chinna*, from √*chid* (cut)

udārāṇām (m. gen. pl.) fully active or engaged, aroused; *ud* (up, forth, out) + *āra*, from √*ṛ* (go) [end of DV cpd.]

Ignorance is the origin of the others, whether dormant, attenuated, interrupted, or fully active.

5. *anitya-aśuci-duḥkha-anātmasu nitya-śuci-sukha-ātma-khyātir avidyā*

anitya (m.) non eternal, temporal, fleeting, transient; *a* (not) + *nitya* (eternal) from √*ni* (lend)

aśuci (m.) impure, defiled; *a* (not) + *śuci*, from √*śuc* (gleam)

duḥkha (n.) difficulty, dissatisfaction, sorrow (see I:31) *anātmasu* (m. loc pl.) non self; *an* (not) + ***ātman,*** self, probably from $\sqrt{}$*an* (breathe) [end of DV cpd.]

nitya (m.) eternal (see above)

śuci (m.) pure, undefiled, untainted (see above)

sukha (n.) pleasure, happiness, joy, well-being (see I:33)

ātman (m.) self (see above) [end of DV cpd.]

khyātir (f. nom. sg.) seeing, ascertainment; from $\sqrt{}$***khyā*** (see I:16)

avidyā (f. nom.sg.) ignorance (see II:3)

Ignorance is seeing the noneternal as eternal, the impure as pure, dissatisfaction as pleasure, and the non-self as self.

6. *dṛg-darśana-śaktyor eka ātmatā iva asmitā*

dṛg (dṛś) (m.) seeing, looking, discerning; from $\sqrt{}$*dṛś (see)*

darśana (m.) what is seen (see I:30)

śaktyor (f. gen. du.) power, ability; from $\sqrt{}$***śak*** (be able) [end of TP6 cpd.]

eka (m.) one

ātmatā (f. nom. sg.) self-ness, nature; from ***ātma*** (self) + *tā*, feminine suffix denoting "having the quality of" [end of KD cpd. meaning "of a single self"]

iva (ind.) as if

asmitā (f. nom. sg.) I-am-ness (see I:17)

I-am-ness is when the two powers of seer and seen [appear] as a single self.

7. *sukha-anuśayī rāgaḥ*

sukha (n.) pleasant (see I:33)

anuśayī (m. nom.sg.) clinging to, resting on; ***anu*** (along, after) + *śaya,* from $\sqrt{}$*śī* (rest) + *in,* possessive suffix [end of TP7 cpd.]

rāgaḥ (m. nom. sg.) attraction (see I:37)

Attraction is clinging to pleasure.

8. *duḥkha-anuśayī dveṣaḥ*

duḥkha (n.) dissatisfaction (see I:31)

anuśayī (m. nom. sg.) clinging to (see above) [end of TP7 cpd.]

dveṣaḥ (m. nom. sg.) aversion (see II:8)

Aversion is clinging to dissatisfaction.

9. *svarasa-vāhī viduṣo' pi tathā ruḍho' bhiniveśaḥ*

svarasa (m.) own inclination; literally own juice or essence; *sva* (self) + *rasa*, from √*ras* (taste)

vāhī (m. nom. sg.) sustained, borne, carried; from √*vah* (carry, flow, sustain)

viduṣo (m. gen. sg.) wise person, sage, one wo knows; from √*vid* (know)

api (ind.) even, also

tathā(ind.) thus

rūdhaḥ (m. nom. sg.) arisen, sprung up, produced from, from √*ruh* (rise, spring up)

abhiniveśaḥ (m. nom. sg.) desire for continuity (see II:3)

Desire for continuity, arising even among the wise, is sustained by self-inclination [i.e., self-sustaining].

10. *te pratiprasava-heyāḥ sūkṣmāḥ*

te (m. nom. pl.) they (refers to afflictions)

pratiprasava (m.) disassociation from the creation process, counter-order, return to the original state, inverse propagation; *prati* (against, back) + *prasava* (creation, begetting), from *pra* (before, forward) + *sava* (pressing out), from √*sū* (generate, impel)

heyāḥ(m. nom. pl.) to be avoided, overcome, abandoned, from √*ha* (leave, abandon) [end of TP3 cpd.]

sūkṣmāḥ (m. nom. pl.) subtle (see I:44)

These subtle ones are to be avoided by a return to the origin.

11. *dhyāna-heyās tad-vṛttayaḥ*
dhyāna (m.) meditation (see I:39)
heyās (m. nom. pl.) avoided (see II:10) [end of TP3 cpd.]
tad (n.) that, those
vṛttayaḥ (m. nom. pl.) fluctuations (see I:2) [end of TP6 cpd.]

The fluctuations of them are to be avoided by meditation.

12. *kleśa-mūlaḥ karma-āśayo dṛṣta-adṛṣṭa-janma-vedanīyaḥ*
kleśa (m.) affliction (see I:24)
mūlaḥ (m. nom. sg.) root, foundation, from $\sqrt{}$*mūl* (be rooted) [end of TP6 cpd.]
karma (n.) action (see I:24)
āśayaḥ (m. nom. sg.) residue (see I.24) [end of TP6 cpd.]
dṛṣta (m.) seen (see I.15)
adṛṣṭa (m.) unseen (see I.15)
janma (n.) existence, life, birth; from $\sqrt{}$*jan* (be born, come into existence)
vedanīyaḥ (m. nom. sg.) to be felt or experienced; gerundive form of $\sqrt{}$*vid* (know) [end of TP6 cpd.]

The residue of karma, rooted in affliction, is felt in seen or unseen existence.

13. *sati mūle tad-vipāko jāty-āyur-bhogāḥ*
sati (m. loc. sg.) being, existing, occuring
mūle (m. loc. sg.) root (see II:12) [end of locative absolute construction]
tad (n.) that
vipākaḥ (m. nom. sg.) fruition (see I.24)
jāti (f.) birth, production, position assigned by caste or rank; from $\sqrt{}$*jan* (be born)
āyur (n.) life, vital power, span of life; *ā* (hither, unto) + *yuḥ*, from $\sqrt{}$*i* (go)

bhogāḥ (m. nom. pl.) experience, enjoyment, eating; from √*bhuj* (enjoy) [end of DV cpd.]

While the root exists, there is fruition of it as birth, duration, and experience.

14. *te hlāda-paritāpa-phalāḥ puṇya-apuṇya-hetutvāt*

te (m. nom. pl.) they, these

hlāda (m.) joyful, delightful, pleasurable; from √*hlād* (rejoice)

paritāpa (m.) pain, agony, grief, sorrow; *pari* (around) + *tāpa*, from √*tap* (be hot) [end of DV cpd.]

phalāḥ (m. nom. pl.) fruits, consequence, result (used adjectively to describe the three life states in II:13) [end of BV cpd.]

puṇya (n.) meritorious, auspicious, propitious, pure, holy, sacred; from √*puṇ* (do good)

apuṇya (n.) opposite of above; *a* (not) + √*puṇ* (do good)

hetutvāt (m. abl. sg.) cause, motive, reason; *hetu*, from √*hi* (impel, incite) + *tva*, suffix indicating quality [end of KD cpd.]

These fruits are joyful or painful according to whether the causes are meritorious or demeritorious.

15. *pariṇāma-tāpa-saṃskāra-duḥkhair guṇa-vṛtti-virodhāc ca duḥkham eva sarvaṃ vivekinaḥ*

pariṇāma (m.) change, alteration, transformations, evolution, development, ripeness, result; *pari* (around) + √*nam* (bow)

tāpa (m.) sorrow, anxiety, pain, *angst*, anguish; √*tap* (be hot)

saṃskāra (m.) impression left by past action (see I:14) [end of TP5 cpd.]

duḥkhair (n. instr. pl.) by dissatisfactions (see I:31) [end of

TP5 cpd.]

guṇa (m.) strand, thread, quality (see I:16)

vṛtti (f.) fluctuation (see I:2)

virodhāt (m. abl. sg.) conflict, opposition, hostility, adversity; *vi* (asunder, away) + *rodha* (obstruct, arrest) [end of TP6 cpd.]

ca (ind.) and

duḥkham (n. nom. sg.) dissatisfaction (see I:31)

eva (ind.) indeed, thus

sarvaṃ (n. nom. sg.) all, everything

vivekinaḥ (m. gen. sg.) discrimination, discerning; *vi* (asunder, away) + *vekin*, from √*vic* (divide asunder, distinguish, sift) + *in*, possessive suffix

For the discriminating one, all is dissatisfaction, due to the conflict of the fluctuations of the *guṇas* and by the dissatisfaction due to *pariṇāma*, sorrow, and *saṃskāra*.

16. *heyaṃ duḥkhaṃ anāgataṃ*

heyaṃ (n. nom. sg.) to be avoided (see II:20)

duḥkham (n. nom. sg.) dissatisfaction (see I:31)

anāgataṃ (n. nom. sg.) not yet come; *an* (not) + *ā* (unto) + *gata* (gone), from √*gam* (go)

The dissatisfaction yet to come is to be avoided.

17. *draṣṭṛ-dṛśyayoḥ saṃyogo heya-hetuḥ*

draṣṭṛ (m.) seer (see I:3)

dṛśyayoḥ (m. gen. du.) seen, that which is visible; from √*dṛś* (see) [end of DV cpd.]

saṃyogaḥ (m. nom. sg.) union, correlation, joining, conjunction; *sam* (together) + *yoga* (union, from √*yuj* (unite, yoke)

heya (n.) to be avoided (see II:20)

hetuḥ (m. nom. sg.) cause, motive, reason; from √*hi* (impel, incite) [end of KD cpd.]

The cause of what is to be avoided is the union of the seer with the seen.

18. *prakāśa-kriyā-sthiti-śīlaṃ bhūta-indriya-ātmakaṃ bhoga-apavargārthaṃ dṛśyaṃ*

prakāśa (m.) light, luster, splendor, brightness; *pra* (before, forward) + *kāśa*, from √*kāś* (shine, appear)

kriyā (f.) activity (see I:1)

sthiti (f.) remaining inert, standing (see I:13) [end of DV cpd.]

śīlam (n. nom. sg.) quality, character, nature; from √*śīl* (serve, act) [end of TP6 cpd.]

bhūta (m.) elements: earth, water, fire, air, space; constituent of the manifest world; from √*bhū* (be)

indriya (n.) sense organ; power; derived from the name Indra [end of DV cpd.]

ātmakaṃ (n. nom. sg.) having the self-nature of; *ātma* (self) + *ka*, possessive suffix

bhoga (m.) experience, enjoyment (see II.13)

apavarga (m.) liberation, emancipation; *apa* (away, off) + *varga*, from *vṛj* (twist, bend, turn) [end of DV cpd.]

arthaṃ (n. nom. sg.) purpose (see I:28) [end of TP6 cpd.]

dṛśyam (n. nom. sg.) seen (see II:17)

The seen has the qualities of light, activity, and inertia*, consists of the elements and senses, and has the purposes of experience and liberation.

* These correspond to the three *guṇas: sattva, rajas, tamas*, respectively.

19. *viśeṣa-aviśeṣa-liṅga-mātra-aliṅgāni guṇa-parvāṇi*

viśeṣa (m.) distinct (see I:22)

aviśeṣa (m.) indistinct; *a* (not) + *viśeṣa* (see I:22)

liṅga (n.) designator, signifier, indicator; from √*liṅg* (paint, mark)
mātra (n.) suffix designating measure or quantity; entirely, only; from √*mā* (measure)
aliṅgāni (n. nom. pl.) literally, without mark; unmanifest; *a* (not) + *liṅga* (see above) [end of DV cpd]
guṇa (m.) thread of strand (see I:16)
parvāṇi (n. nom. pl.) division, level; from √*pṛ* (fill) [end of TP6 cpd.]

The distinct, the indistinct, the designator, and the unmanifest are the divisions of the *guṇas*.

According to Vyāsa, these four divisions are as follows: The distinct (*viśeṣa*) has sixteen parts: five gross elements (space, air, fire, water, earth), the five sense organs (ears, skin, eyes, tongue, nose), the five action organs (mouth, hands, feets, and organs of evacuation and generation), and the mind. The indistinct (*aviśeṣa*) includes six parts: the five subtle elements (hearing, touching, seeing, tasting, smelling) and the sense of self (*ahaṃkāra*). The designator (*liṅga-mātra*) is the intellect (*buddhi*) and the unmanifest *aliṅga* is *mūlaprakṛti*.

20. *draṣṭā dṛśi-mātraḥ śuddho'pi pratyaya-anupaśyaḥ*
draṣṭā (m. nom. sg.) seer (see I:3)
dṛśi (f.) seeing, power of seeing; from √*dṛś* (see)
mātraḥ (m. nom. sg.) only (see II:20)
śuddhaḥ (m. nom. sg.) pure, correct, cleansed; from √*śudh* (purify, clean)
api (ind.) also, even; although
pratyaya (m.) intention (see I:10)
anupaśyaḥ (m. nom. sg.) to appear, to be looked upon, to be taken as *anu* (along, after) + *paśya* from √*paś* (see) [end of T6 cpd.]

The seer only sees; though pure, it appears intentional.

21. *tad-artha eva dṛśyaya-ātmā*
tad (n.) that, this; in this case refers to the seer *(puruṣa)*
arthaḥ (m. nom. sg.) purpose (see I:28) [end of TP6 cpd.]
eva (ind.) indeed, only
dṛśyaya (m. gen. sg.) seen (see II.17)
ātmā (m. nom. sg.) nature, self, essence; (see II:5)

The nature of the seen is only for the purpose of that *(puruṣa)*.

22. *kṛta-arthaṃ prati naṣṭam apy anaṣṭam tad anya-sādhāraṇatvāt*
kṛta (m.) done, made; from √*kṛ* (do, make)
arthaṃ (n. nom. sg.) purpose (see I:s8) [end of KD cpd.]
prati (ind.) towards, for.
naṣṭa (n. nom. sg.) disappeared, lost, destroyed, expelled, wasted; from √*naś* (perish)
api (ind.) even, also
anaṣṭam (n. nom. sg.) not destroyed; *a* (not) + *naṣṭam* (see above)
tad (n.) that
anya (n.) other
sādhāraṇatvāt (n. abl. sg.) commonality, universality; *sā* (with) + *dhāraṇa* (holding), from √*dhṛ* (hold) [end of TP6 cpd.]

When (its) purpose is done, it disappears; otherwise it does not disappear due to being common to others.

23. *sva-svāmi-śaktyoḥ sva-rūpa-upalabdhi-hetuḥ saṃyogaḥ*
sva (m.) owned
svāmi (m.) owner, lord, chief
śaktyoḥ (f. gen. du:) power (see II:6)
svarūpa (n.) own form (see I:3)
upalabdhi (f.) apprehension, perception; *upa* (to, unto)

labdhi, from $\sqrt{labh}$ (obtain)
hetuḥ (m. nom. sg.) cause (see II:17)
saṃyogaḥ (m. nom. sg.) union (see II:17)

Union *(saṃyoga)* is the cause of apprehending as [one] self-form the two powers of owner and owned.

24. *tasya hetur avidyā*
tasya (m. gen. sg.) of it
hetuḥ (m. nom. sg.) cause (see II:17)
avidyā (f. nom. sg.) ignorance (see II:3)

The cause of it is ignorance.

25. *tad-abhāvāt saṃyoga-abhāvo hānaṃ tad-dṛśeḥ kaivalyaṃ*
tad (n.) that (refers to ignorance)
abhāvāt (m. abl. sg.) absence, nonexistence, negation; *a* (not) + *bhāva* (being), from $\sqrt{bh\bar{u}}$ (be); see I:10
saṃyoga (m.) union (see II:17)
abhāvaḥ (m. nom. sg.) see above [end of TP6 cpd.]
hānaṃ (n. nom. sg.) escape, giving up, relinquishment; abandoning; cessation; from $\sqrt{h\bar{a}}$ (depart)
tad (n.) that
dṛśeḥ (f. abl. sg.) from the seen (see II: 20)
kaivalyaṃ (n. nom. sg.) isolation, aloneness; single unitary, uncompounded; from the noun *kevala*, meaning alone, not connected to anything

From its absence, union *(saṃyoga)* ceases; [this is] the escape, the isolation from the seen.

26. *viveka-khyātir aviplavā hānopāyaḥ*
viveka (m.) discrimination, discerning (see II:15)
khyātir (f. nom. sg.) discernment, perception, knowledge (see

I:16) [end of KD cpd.]

aviplavā (f. nom. sg.) unfaltering, unbroken, unwavering; *a* (not) + *vi* as (asunder, away) +*plava*, from √*plu* (float)

hāna (n.) escape (see I:25)

upāyaḥ (m. nom. sg.) means, method, that by which one reaches a goal; *upa* (to, unto), + *aya*, from √*i* (go)

The means of escape is unfaltering discriminative discernment.

27. *tasya saptadhā prānta-bhūmiḥ prajñā*

tasya (m. gen. sg.) of him (the accomplished Yogin)

saptadhā (f. nom. sg.) sevenfold; *sapta* (seven) +*dhā*, suffix fold

prānta (m.) last, edge, boundary; *pra* (before, forward) + *anta* (end, limit)

bhumiḥ (f. nom. sg.) stage, place (see I:14) [end of KD cpd.]

prajñā (f. nom. sg.) wisdom (see I:20)

His wisdom to the last stage is seven-fold.

According to Vyāsa, the seven stages are 1) that which is to be known has been known; 2) that which is to be avoided has been avoided; 3) that which is to be attained has been attained; 4) the means (discriminative discernment) has been realized; 5) the intellect has completed its purpose of providing experience and liberation; 6) the activities of the *guṇas* have ceased; 7) *puruṣa* abides in isolation.

28. *yoga-aṅga-anuṣṭhānād aśuddhi-kṣaye jñāna-dīptir ā viveka-khyāteḥ*

yoga (m.) (see I:1)

aṅga (n.) limb, member, division, body (see I:31)

anuṣṭhānād (n. abl. sg.) following, carring out, undertaking, doing; *anu* (along, after) + *sthāna*, from √*sthā* (stand) [end of TP6 cpd.]

aśuddhi (f.) impure, sullied; *a* (not) + *śuddhi*, from √*śudh* (purify)

kṣaye (m. loc. sg.) destruction, loss, wearing away: from √*kṣi* (destroy)

jñāna (m.) knowledge (see I:8)

dīptir (f. nom. sg.) light, splendor, radiance; from √*dīp* (to light)

ā (ind.) up to, as far as

viveka (m.) discrimination (see II:15)

khyāteḥ (f. abl. sg.) discernment (see I:16)

From following the limbs of yoga, on the destruction of impurity there is a light of knowledge, leading to discriminative discernment.

29. *yama-niyama-āsana-prāṇāyāma-pratyāhāra-dhāraṇā-dhyāna-samādhayo, stāv-aṅgāni*

yama (m.) restraint, self-control, holding back; from √*yam* (restrain)

niyama (m.) observance; *ni* (down, into) + √*yam* (restrain)

āsana (n.) posture, position, sitting down; from √*ās* (sit, be)

prāṇāyāma (m.) control of breath; *prāṇa* (breath) from *pra* (before, forward) + √*an* (breathe) + *yāma*, from √*yam* (see above)

pratyāhāra (m.) withdrawal, retreat, holding back (especially of senses); *prati* (against, back) +*ā* (unto) +hāra, from √*hṛ* (take, hold)

dhāraṇā (f.) concentration, act of holding, retaining; from √*dhṛ* (hold, maintain)

dhyāna (n.) meditation (see I:39)

samādhayaḥ (m. nom. pl.) absorption, concentration, unified state of awareness (see I:20) [end of DV cpd.]

aṣṭau (m.) eight

aṅgāni (n. nom. pl.) limb (see II:28)

Restraint, observances, postures, control of breath, withdrawal, concentration, meditation, and *samādhi* are the eight limbs.

30. *ahiṃsā-satya-asteya-brahmacarya-aparigrahā yamāḥ*

ahiṃsā (f.) nonviolence; absence of desire to kill or injure; *a* (not) *+himsā*, desiderative derivative from $\sqrt{han}$ (strike, kill)

satya (n.) authenticity, truthfulness, sincerity, veracity; from *sat* (real, actual), present participle of $\sqrt{as}$ (be, exist)

asteya (n.) not stealing; *a* (not) *+steya*, from $\sqrt{stai}$ (steal)

brahmacarya (n.) sexual restraint, chastity, continence; *brahma* (one versed in sacred knowledge) *+carya*, engaged in, from $\sqrt{car}$ (move, walk)

aparigrahāḥ (m. nom. pl.) nonpossession, renunciation of nonessentials; *a* (not) + *pari* (around) + *graha* (holding), from $\sqrt{grabh}$ (grasp, hold) [end of DV cpd.]

yamāḥ (m. nom. pl.) restraint (see II:29)

The restraints are nonviolence, truthfulness, nonstealing, sexual restraint, and nonpossession.

31. *jāti-deśa-kāla-samaya-anavacchinnāḥ sarva-bhaumā mahāvratam*

jāti (f.) birth (see II:13)

deśa (m.) place, region. location; from $\sqrt{diś}$ (point out)

kāla (m.) time (see I:26)

samaya (m.) circumstance, coming together; *sam* (together) + *aya*, from $\sqrt{i}$ (go) [end of DV cpd.)

anavacchināḥ (m. nom. pl.) unlimited, unbounded, not delineated; *an* (not) + *ava* (down)+ *chinna*, from *chid* (cut) [end of TP3 cpd.]

sārva (m.) all, every; strengthened form of *sarva*
bhaumāḥ (m. nom. pl.) occasion, anything related to the world or earth; strengthened form of *bhūmi* (earth) [end of BV cpd.]
mahā (m.) great, large, extensive
vratam (n. nom. sg.) vow, resolve, conduct, decision; from √*vṛ* (choose, decide) [end of KD cpd.]

When not limited by birth, place, time, or circumstance in all occasions [these constitute] the great vow.

32. *śauca-saṃtoṣa-tapaḥ-svādhyāya-īśvara-praṇidhānāni niyamāḥ*
śauca (n.) purity, cleanliness; strengthened form of *śuci* (see II:5)
saṃtoṣa (m.) contentment, satisfaction; *sam* (together) + *toṣa* from √*tuṣ* (enjoy)
tapaḥ (n.) austerity (see II:1)
svādhyāya (m.) self-study (see II:1)
īśvara (m.) (see I:23)
praṇidhānāni (n. nom. pl.) dedication (see I:23)
niyamāḥ (m. nom. pl.) observance (see II:29)

Purity, contentment, austerity, self-study, and dedication to Īśvara are the observances.

33. *vitarka-bādhane pratipakṣa-bhāvanam*
vitarka (m.) discursive thought (see I:17)
bādhane (m. loc. sg.) bondage, inhibiting, binding; from √*bādh* (harass, oppress, trouble) [end] of TP5 cpd.]
pratipakṣa (m.) opposite; *prati* (against, back) +*pakṣa* (wing)
bhāvanam (n. nom. sg.) cultivation (see I:28) [end of TP6 cpd.]

When there is bondage due to discursive thought, the cultivation of

the opposite [is prescribed].

34. *vitarkā hiṃsā-ādayaḥ kṛta-kārita-anumoditā lobha-krodha-moha-pūrvakā mṛdu-madhya-adhimātrā duḥkha-ajñāna-ananta-phalā iti pratipakṣa-bhāvanam*

vitarkāḥ (m. nom. sg.) discursive thought (see I:17)
hiṃsā (f.) violence (see II:30)
ādayaḥ (m. nom. pl.) and the rest, starting with; *etcetera;* from *ādi*
kṛta (m.) done, make (see II:22)
kārita (m.) caused to be done; from √*kṛ* (do)
anumoditāḥ (m. nom. pl.) approved, permitted; *anu* (along, after) +*modita*, from √*mud* (rejoice, celebrate) [end of DV cpd.]
lobha (m.) lust, greed, cupidity; from √*lubh* (entice, allure)
krodha (m.) anger, wrath, passion; from √*krudh* (be angry)
moha (m.) delusion, bewilderment, perplexity; from √*muh* (be stupefied)
pūrvakāḥ (m. nom. pl.) consisting of, accompanied by, connected with; *pūrva* (prior) + *ka* (nominalizing suffix) [end of TP3 cpd.]
mṛdu (m.) mild (see I:22)
madhya (m.) medium (see I:22)
adhimātrāḥ (m. nom. pl.) intense (see I:22) [end of DV cpd.]
duḥkha (n.) dissatisfaction (see I:31)
ajñāna (n.) ignorance; *a* (not) +*jñāna* (see I.8)
ananta (m.) boundless, endless, eternal, infinite
phalāh (m. nom. pl.) fruits (see II:14) [end of BV cpd.]
iti (ind.) thus, so
pratipakṣa (m.) opposite (see II:33)
bhāvanam (n. nom. sg.) cultivation (see I:28) [end of TP6 cpd.]

Discursive thoughts like violence, etc., whether done, caused, or approved, consisting of lust, anger, or delusion, and whether mild,

medium or intense, have as their endless fruits dissatisfaction and ignorance; thus, cultivation of opposites [is prescribed].

35. *ahiṃsā-pratiṣṭāyāṃ tat-saṃnidhau vaira-tyāgaḥ*
ahiṃsā (f.) nonviolence (see II:30)
pratiṣṭhāyāṃ (f. loc. sg.) established, abiding, standing; *prati* (against, back) + *ṣṭhāyam*, from √*sthā* (stand) [end of TP7 cpd.]
tat (n.) that
saṃnidhau (m. loc. sg.) presence, nearness, proximity; *sam* (together) + *ni* (down, into) + *dhi*, from √*dhā* (put, place) [end of TP6 cpd.]
vaira (m.) hostility, animosity, enmity; from *vīra* (vehemence)
tyāgaḥ (m. nom. sg.) abandonment, leaving behind, giving up; from √*tyaj* (renounce) [end of TP6 cpd.]

When in the presence of one established in nonviolence, there is the abandonment of hostility.

36. *satya-pratiṣṭhāyāṃ kriyā-phala-āśrayatvam*
satya (n.) truthfulness (see II:30)
pratiṣṭhāyām (f. loc. sg.) established (see II:35) [end of TP7 cpd.]
kriyā (f.) action (see II:1)
phala (n.) fruit (see II:14)
āśrayatvam (n. nom. sg.) correspondence; dwelling in, depending on, following; ā (hither, unto) + *śraya* protection, refuge; from √*śri* (rest on) + *tva*, suffix denoting "ness" [end of TP3 cpd.]

When established in truthfulness, [there is] correspondence between action and fruit.

37. *asteya-pratiṣṭhāyaṃ sarva-ratna-upasthānam*

asteya (n.) not stealing (see II:30)
pratisthāyām (f. loc. sg.) established (see II:34)
sarva (n.) all *ratna* (n.) jewel, gem
upasthānam (n. nom. sg.) presence, appearance; *upa* (to, unto) + *sṭḥāna*, from √*stha* (stand) [end of TP6 cpd.]

When established in nonstealing, [whatever is] present is all jewels.

38. *brahmacarya-pratiṣṭhāyaṃ vīrya-lābhaḥ*
brahmacarya (n.) sexual restraint (see II:30)
pratiṣṭhāyāṃ (f. loc. sg.) established (see II:34) [end of TP7 cpd.]
vīrya (n.) vigor, strength, power, energy; from √*vīr* (be powerful)
labhaḥ (m. nom. sg.) obtained, gotten; from √*labh* (obtain) [end of TP6 cpd.]

When established in sexual restraint, vigor is obtained.

39. *aparigraha-sthairye janma-kathaṃtā saṃbodhaḥ*
aparigraha (m.) nonpossession (see II:30)
sthairye (n. loc. sg.) steadfastness, firmness, stability; from √*sthā* (stand) [end of TP7 cpd.]
janma (n.) existence, birth, origin (see II:12)
kathaṃtā (f. nom. sg.) the how or what; whatness: *katham* (how) + *tā*, feminine suffix denoting quality
saṃbodhaḥ (m. nom. sg.) knowledge, understanding: *sam* (together) +*bodha*, from √*budh* (awaken)

When steadfast in nonpossession, there is knowledge of "the how" of existence.

40. *śaucāt sva-aṅga-jugupsā parair asaṃsargaḥ*
śauca (n.) purity (see II:32)

sva (m.) own
aṅga (n.) body, limb, member (see I:31)
jugupsā (f. nom. sg.) dislike, disgust; reduplicated desiderative form of $\sqrt{}$*gup* (shun, avoid)
parair (m. instr. pl.) others
asaṃsargaḥ (m. nom. sg.) noncontact, nonassociation; *a* (not) + *sam* (together) + *sarga*, from $\sqrt{}$*sṛj* (emit)

From purity arises dislike for one's own body and noncontact with others.

41. *sattva-śuddhi-saumanasya-eka-agrya-indriya-jaya-ātma-darśana-yogyatvāni ca*
sattva (n.) lightness, "being-ness," existence; *sat* (existence) + *tva*, suffix indicating quality
śuddhi (f.) purity (see II:28) [end of KD cpd.]
saumanasya (m.) cheerfulness, gladness, satisfaction of mind; *sau* strengthened form of *su* (goodness) + *manasya* (to have in mind)
eka (m.) one
agrya (m.) intent, closely attentive; from *agra* (foremost) [end of TP6 cpd.]; with *eka*, one pointedness
indriya (n.) sense organ (see II:18)
jaya (m.) mastery, conquering, being victorious; from $\sqrt{}$*ji* (conquer) [end of TP6 cpd.]
ātman (m.) self (see II:5)
darśana (m.) vision, view (see I:30) [end of TP6 cpd.]
yogyatvāni (n. nom. pl.) fitness, suitability, ability; *yogya*, from $\sqrt{}$*yuj* (join) +*tva*, suffix indicating quality [end of DV cpd.]
ca (ind.) and

And purity of *sattva*, cheerfulness, one pointedness, mastery of the senses, and fitness for the vision of the self.

42. *saṃtoṣād anuttamaḥ sukha-lābhaḥ*
saṃtoṣād (m. abl. sg.) contentment (see II:32)
anuttamaḥ(m. nom. sg.) unsurpassed, excellent; *an* (not) + *ud* (up) + *tama*, suffix forming superlative
sukha (n.) happiness, joy (see I:33)
lābhaḥ (m. nom. sg.) obtained, gained (see II:38)

From contentment, unsurpassed happiness is obtained.

43. *kāya-indriya-siddhir aśuddhi-kṣayāt tapasaḥ*
kāya (m.) body, assemblage; from √*ci* (gather)
indriya (n.) sense organ (see II:18)
siddhir (f. nom. sg.) perfection, accomplishment, attainment; from √*sidh* (accomplish) [end of TP7 cpd.]
aśuddhi (f.) impure (see II:28)
kṣayāt (m. abl. sg.) destruction (see II:28)
tapasaḥ (n. abl. sg.) austerity (see II:1)

From austerity arises the destruction of impurity and the perfection of the body and senses.

44. *svādhyāyād iṣṭa-devatā-saṃprayogaḥ*
svādhyāyād (m. abl. sg.) self-study (see II:1)
iṣṭa (m.) intended, sought, desired, liked; from √*iṣ* (wish)
devatā (f.) god, divinity; *deva* (god) + *tā* feminine suffix denoting quality [end of KD cpd.]
saṃprayogaḥ (m. nom. sg.) union, joining together; *sam* (together) +*pra* (before) +*yoga*, from √*yuj* (join) [end of TP3 cpd.]

From self study (arises) union with the desired deity.

45. *samādhi-siddhir īśvara-praṇidhānāt*
samādhi (f.) absorption (see I:20)
siddhir (f. nom. sg.) perfection (see II:43) [end of TP6 cpd]

īśvara (m.) (see I:23)
praṇidhānāt (m. abl. sg.) devotion (see I:23) [end of TP4 cpd.]

Perfection in *samādhi* (arises) from dedication to *Īśvara*.

46. *sthira-sukhaṃ āsanam*
sthira (m.) steadiness, firmness; from √*sthā* (stand)
sukhaṃ (n. nom. sg.) ease (see I:33)
āsanam (n. nom. sg.) posture (see II:29)

***Āsana* is steadiness and ease,**

47. *prayatna-śaithilya-ananta-samāpattibhyām*
prayatna (m.) effort, striving, exertion; *pra* (before, forward) + *yatna*, from √*yat* (strive)
śaithilya (n.) relaxation, looseness; from √*śratu* (untie, loosen)
ananta (m.) endless (see II:34)
samāpattibhyām (f. abl. du.) unity (see I:41)

From relaxation of effort and endless unity.

48. *tato dvandva-anabhighātāḥ*
tatas (ind.) thus, from that
dvandva (n.) pair of opposites; literally, "two-two"
anabhigātāḥ (n. nom. pl.) assault, attacking, assailing; *an* (not) + *abhi* (to, unto) *ghāta*, from √*han* (strike, kill) [end of TP3 cpd.]

Thus, there is no assault by the pairs of opposites.

49. *tasmin sati śvāsa-praśvāsayor gati-vicchedaḥ prāṇāyāmaḥ*
tasmin (m. loc. sg.) in this
sati (m. loc. sg.) being (see II:13)

śvāsa (m.) breath, in breath; from √*śvas* (breathe)
praśvasayoḥ (m. gen. du.) outbreath, exhalation; *pra* (before, forward) + *śvasa* (see above) [end of DV cpd.]
gati (f.) notion, procession; from √*gam* (go)
vicchedaḥ (m. nom. sg.) cutting off, breaking; *vi* (away, asunder) + *cheda*, from √*chid* (cut) [end of TP6 cpd.]
prāṇāyāmaḥ (m. nom. sg.) control of breath (see II:29)

Being in this, there is control of breath, which is the cutting off of the motion of in breath and out breath.

50. *bāhya-abhyantara-stambha-vṛttir deśa-kala-saṃkhyābhiḥ paridṛṣṭo dīrgha-sūkṣmaḥ*
bāhya (m.) external, outer; from *bahis* (outside)
abhyantara (m.) internal, inside; *abhi* (to, unto) + *antar* (interior, inside)
stambha (m.) suppressed, stopped, obstructed ; from √*stambh* (hold up) [end of DV cpd.]
vṛttir (f. nom. sg.) fluctuation (see I:2) [end of KD cpd.]
deśa (m.) place (see II:31)
kāla (m.) time (see I:14)
saṃkhyābhis (f. instr. pl.) observation, calculation; *sam* (together) + √*khyā* (count) [end of TP6 cpd.]
paridṛṣto (m. nom. sg.) seen beheld, perceived; *pari* (around) + *dṛṣta*, from √*dṛś* (see)
dīrgha (m.) long, lofty, tall
sūkṣmaḥ (m. nom. sg.) subtle (see I:44) [end of DV cpd.]

Its fluctuations are external, internal, and suppressed; it is observed according to time, place, and number, and becomes long and subtle.

51. *bāhya-abhyantara-viṣaya-ākṣepī caturthaḥ*
bāhya (m.) external (see II:50)
abhyantara (m.) internal (see II:50) [end of DV cpd.]

viṣaya (m.) condition (see I:11) [end of KD cpd.]
ākṣepī (n. nom sg.) withdrawal, casting aside; *a* (hither, unto) +*kṣepin*, from √*kṣip* (throw, cast) + possessive suffix *in* [end of TP] cpd.]
caturthaḥ (m. nom. sg.) fourth

The fourth is withdrawal from external and internal conditions [of breath].

52. *tataḥ kṣīyate prakāśa-āvaraṇam*
tataḥ (ind.) then
kṣīyate (3rd pers. sg. pass.) is dissolved, destroyed, diminished; class I verb √*kṣi* (destroy)
prakāśa (m.) light, clearness, brightness, splendor; *pra* (before, forward) + *kāśa*, (shine) (see II:18)
āvaraṇam (n. nom. sg.) covering, concealing; *a* (hither, unto) +*varaṇa*, from √*vṛ* (cover) [end of TP6 cpd.]

Then the covering of light is dissolved.

53.*dhāraṇāsu ca yogyatāmanasaḥ*
dhāranāsu (f. loc. pl.) in concentrations (see II:29)
ca (ind.) and
yogyatā (f. nom. sg.) fitness (see II:41)
manasaḥ (n. gen. sg.) of the mind (see I:35)

And there is fitness of the mind-organ for concentrations.

54. *sva-viṣaya-asaṃprayoge cittasya sva-rūpa-anukāra iva indriyāṇaṃ pratyāhāraḥ*
sva (m.) own (see I:3)
viṣaya (m.) circumstance, object (see I:11)
asaṃprayoge (n. loc. sg.) disengagement; *a* (not) + *saṃprayoga* (see II:44)
cittasya (n. gen. sg.) of mind (see I:2)

sva (m.) own (see I:3)
rūpa (n.) form (see I:3)
anukāraḥ (n. nom. sg.) imitation, resemblance: *anu* (along, after) + *kāra*, from √*kṛ* (do)
iva (ind.) as if, just as
indriyāṇāṃ (n. gen. pl.) of the senses (see II:18)
pratyāhāraḥ (m. nom sg.) withdrawal (see II:29)

Withdrawal of the senses is the disengagement from conditions as if in imitation of the own-form of the mind.

The senses follow the course of the mind *(citta)*. When the mind withdraws from sensory activity the senses are also withdraws

55. *tataḥ paramā vaśyatā indriyāṇām*

tataḥ (ind.) then
paramā (f. nom. sg.) utmost, best; superlative form of *para*
vaśyatā (f. nom sg.) command, control, being subdued or subjected; *vaśya*, from √*vaś* (will, command) + *tā*, feminine suffix meaning quality
indriyāṇām (n. gen. pl.) senses (see II:18)

Then arises utmost command of the senses.

III: *Vibhūti-pāda*

1. *deśa-bandhaś cittasya dhāraṇā*
   deśa (m.) place (see I:31)
   bandhaḥ (m. nom. sg.) binding, holding; from √*bandh* (bind) [end of TP7 cpd.]
   cittasya (m. gen. sg.) mind (see I:2)
   dhāraṇā (f. nom. sg.) concentration (see II:29)

Concentration of the mind is (its) binding to a place.

2. *tatra pratyaya-eka-tānatā dhyānam*
   tatra (ind.) there (see I:13)
   pratyaya (m.) intention (see I:10)
   eka (m.) one (see I:32)
   tānatā (f. nom. sg.) extension, stretching; *tāna*, from √*tan* (extend), + *tā* (feminine suffix denoting "having the quality of")
   dhyānam (n. nom. sg.) meditation (see (I:39)

The extension of one intention there is meditation.

3. *tad eva-artha-mātra-nirbhāsaṃ svarūpa-śūnyam iva samādhiḥ*
   tad (n. nom. sg.) that
   eva (ind.) indeed
   artha (m. or n.) purpose, meaning (see I:28)
   mātra (m.) only (see I:43)
   nirbhāsaṃ (n. nom. sg.) shining forth (see I:43)
   śūnyaṃ (n. nom. sg.) empty (see I:9)
   iva (ind.) as if
   samādhiḥ (f. nom. sg.) absorption (see I:20)

When the purpose alone shines forth as if empty of own form, that indeed is *samādhi*.

When one realizes through meditation that all objects and conditions are presented for the sake of *puruṣa, samādhi* arises. In this *sūtra*, purpose refers to any interded object (see I:43).

4. *trayam ekatra saṃyamaḥ*
   trayam (n. nom. sg.) threesome
   ekatra (ind.) in one, in one and the same together; from *eka* (one)
   saṃyamaḥ (m. nom. sg.) binding together, holding, restraint, control; *sam* (together) + *yama*, from $\sqrt{yam}$ (restrain)

The unity of these three is *saṃyama*.

5. *taj-jayāt prajñā ālokaḥ*
   tad (n.) that
   jayāt (m. abl. sg.) mastery (see II:41) (end of TP6 cpd.)
   prajñā (f. nom. sg.) wisdom (see I:20)
   ālokaḥ (m. nom. sg.) light, lustre, splendor; *ā* (hither, unto) + *lokaḥ* (world), from $\sqrt{lok}$ (see, behold) (end of TP6 cpd.)

From the mastery of that, the splendor of wisdom.

6. *tasya bhūmiṣu viniyogaḥ*
   tasya (m. gen. sg.) of it
   bhumiṣu (m. loc. sg.) stage (see I:14)
   viniyogaḥ (m. nom. sg.) application, progression; *vi* (asunder, away), + *ni* (down, into), + *yoga* (see I:1)

Its application is in stages.

7. *trayam-antar-aṅgaṃ pūrvebhyaḥ*
trayam (n. nom. sg.) threesome (see III:4)
   antar (ind.) inner
   aṅgaṃ (n. nom. sg.) limb (see I:31)
   pūrvebhyaḥ (m. abl. pl.) prior (see I:18)

These three inner limbs are (distinct) from the prior ones.

8. *tad api bahir-aṅgaṃ nirbījasya*
tad (n. nom. sg.) that
api (ind.) indeed, also
bahir (ind.) outer, external
aṅgaṃ (n. nom. sg.) limb (see I:31)
nirbījasya (m. gen. sg.) seedless (see I:51)

These indeed are outer limbs [in regard to] the seedless.

9. *vyutthāna-nirodha-saṃskārayor abhibhava-prādurbhāvau nirodha-kṣaṇa-citta-anvayo nirodha-pariṇāmaḥ*
vyutthāna (m.) emergence, state of being turned outward; *vi* (away, asunder) + *ut* (up) + *thāna*, from √*sthā* (stand)
nirodha (m.) restraint (see I:2)
saṃskārayoḥ (m. gen. du.) (see I:18) [end of TP6 cpd.]
abhibhava (m.) overpowering, powerful; *abhi* (to, toward) + *bhāva*, from √*bhū* (be)
prādurbhavau (m. nom. du.) appearance, manifestation; from *prādur* (bring to light, make manifest or visible) + *bhāva*, from √*bhū* (be)
nirodha (m.) restraint (see I:2)
kṣana (n.) moment, instant
citta (n.) mind (see I:2)
anvayoḥ (m. nom. sg.) following, succession, connection; *anu* (along, after) + *aya*, from √*i* (go)
nirodha (m.) restraint (see I:2)
pariṇāmaḥ (m. nom. sg.) engagement, transformation (see II:15)

[In regard to] the two *saṃskāras* of emergence and restraint, when that of appearance (emergence) is overpowered, there follows a moment of restraint in the mind; this is the *pariṇāma* of restraint.

10. *tasya praśānta vāhitā saṃskārāt*
tasya (m. gen. sg.) of this

praśānta (m.) pacified, calm, quiet, composed; *pra* (before, forward) + *śānta*, from √*śam* (be quiet)

vāhitā (f. nom. sg.) flow; exertion, endeavor; from √*vah* (press) [end of KD cpd.]

saṃskārat (m. abl. sg.) (see I:18)

From the *saṃskāra* of this there is a calm flow.

11. *sarva-arthatā-ekāgratayoḥ kṣaya-udayau cittasya samādhi-pariṇāmaḥ*

sarva (n.) all

arthatā (f.) thingness, objectivity; from *artha* (possession, wealth; see also I:28) + *tā* feminine suffix denoting "having the quality of"

ekāgratayoḥ (f. loc. du.) one-pointedness (see II:41) [end of DV cpd.]

kṣaya (m.) destruction (see II:28)

udayau (m. loc. du.) arisen; *ud* (up) + *aya* from √*i* (go) [end of DV cpd.] (end of locative absolute construction)

cittasya (m. gen. sg.) mind, conciousness (see I:2)

samādhi (f.) (see I:20)

pariṇāmaḥ (m. nom. sg.) engagement, modification (see II:15) [end of TP6 cpd.]

When there is destruction of all objectivity and the arising of one-pointedness, there is of the mind the *pariṇāma* of *samādhi*.

12. *tataḥ punaḥ śānta-uditau tulya-pratyayau cittasya-ekāgratā-pariṇāmah*

tataḥ (ind.) hence

punaḥ (ind.) again, repeated

śānta (m.) quieted, appreased, pacified, calm, undisturbed; from √*śam* (be quiet)

udita (m. nom. du.) uprisen, apparent, visible; *ud* (up) + *ita*, from √*i* (go) [end of DV cpd.]

tulya (m.) same, equal, of the same kind, similar; from √*tul* (weigh)

pratyayau (m. nom. du.) intention (see:I:10) [end of KD cpd.]
cittasya (m. gen. sg.) mind (see I:2)
ekāgratā (f.) one-pointedness (see II:41)
pariṇāmaḥ (m. nom. sg.) engagement, modification, transformation (see II:15) [end of TP6 cpd.]

Hence again, when there is equality between arising and quieted intentions, there is the *pariṇāma* of onepointedness of the mind.

13. *etena bhūta-indriyeṣu dharma-lakṣaṇa-avasthā-pariṇāmā vyā khyātāḥ*
etena (m. instr. sg.) through this (from *etad*)
bhūta (m.) elements (see II:18)
indriyeṣu (m. loc. pl.) senses (see II:18) [end of DV cpd.]
dharma (m.) nature, character, essential quality; that which is established or held; virtue, religion; from √*dhṛ* (hold)
lakṣaṇa (m.) designation, mark, sigh, symbol, definition; from √*lakṣ* (recognize)
avasthā (f.) stability; state, condition; *ava* (down) + √*stha* (stand)
pariṇāmāḥ (m. nom. pl.) engagement (see II:15)
vyākhyātāḥ (m. nom. pl.) explained (see I:44)

By this are similarly explained the *pariṇāmas* of state, designation, and *dharma* amongst the elements and the senses.
These appear to be categorizations of the movements *(pariṇama)* of the three *guṇas* (see II:15). In other words, these three *pariṇāmas* enbody the *guṇa pariṇāma.*

14. *śānta-udita-avyapadeśya-dharma-anupātī-dharmī*
śānta (m.) quieted (see III:12)
udita (m.) arising (see III:12)
avyapadeśya (m.) undetermined, undefined; *a* (not) + *vi* (asunder, away) + *apa* (away, off) + *deśya,* from √*diś* (point out)

[end of DV cpd.]

dharma (m.) (see III:13) [end of KD cpd.]

anupatī (m. nom. sg.) following corresponds to (see I:9) [end of TP7 cpd.]

dharmī (m. nom. sg.) holder of *dharma* (see III:13); *dharma* + *in* (possessive suffix)

The *dharma*-holder corresponds to the *dharma* whether quieted, arisen, or undetermined (past, present, or future).

15. *krama-anyatvaṃ pariṇāma-anyatve hetuḥ*

krama (m.) series, succession, order; from √*kram* (go, walk, step)

anyatvam (n. nom. sg.) otherness; *anya* (other) + *tvam*, neuter suffix denoting having the quality of [end of TP7 cpd.]

pariṇāma (m.) (see II:15)

anyatve (n. loc. sg.) in the otherness or difference (see above) [end of TP6 cpd.]

hetuḥ (n. nom. sg.) cause (see II:17)

The cause of the difference between *pariṇāmas* is the difference in the succession.

16. *pariṇāma-traya-saṃyamād atīta-anāgata-jñānam*

pariṇāma (m.) (see II:15)

traya (m.) threefold (see III:4)

saṃyamād (m. abl. sg.) binding together (see III:4) [end of TP7 cpd.]

atīta (m.) past, from *ati* (over, beyond) + *ita*, past perfect participle of √*i* (go)

anāgata (m.) future, yet to happen; *an* (not) + *ā* (hither, unto) + *gata*, past perfect participle of √*gam* (go)

jñānam (n. nom. sg.) knowledge (see I:8) [end of TP7 cpd.]

From *saṃyama* on the threefold *pariṇāmas* (there is) knowledge of past and future.

17. *śabda-artha-pratyayānām itara-itara adhyāsāt saṃkaras tat pravibhāga-saṃyamāt sarva-bhūta-rūta-jñānam*

śabda (m.) word, sound, noise, voice, speech, language
artha (m. or n.) thing, meaning, aim, purpose (see I:2)
pratyayānām (m. gen. pl.) of the intentions (see I:10) [end of TP7 cpd.]
itara (ind.) whereas
itara (ind.) whereas; when appearing together, they mean "this contrasts with that"
adhyāsāt (m. abl. sg.) imposition, overlapping; *adhi* (over, on) + *āsa*, from $\sqrt{as}$ (be)
saṃkaraḥ (m. nom. sg.) confusion, mixing together, commingling; *sam* (together) + *kara* from $\sqrt{kṛ}$ (scatter)
tat (n. nom. sg.) that
pravibhāga (m.) distinction, separation, division; *pra* (before) + *vi* (asunder) + *bhāga*, from $\sqrt{bhaj}$ (divide)
saṃyamāt (m. abl. sg.) from *saṃyama* (see III:4) [end of TP7 cpd.]
sarva (n.) all (see I:25)
bhūta (m.) being (see II:8)
rūta (n.) utterance, cry, noise, roar, yell, sound; from $\sqrt{ru}$ (roar) [end of TP6 cpd.]
jñānam (n. nom. sg.) knowledge (see I:8) [end of TP6 cpd.]

From the overlapping here and there of words, purposes, and intentions, there is confusion. From *saṃyama* on the distinctions of them, there is knowledge of the (way of) utterance of all beings.
This *sūtra* refers to the way language is generated and understood, (See III:3).

18. *saṃskāra-sākṣāt karaṇāt pūrva-jāti-jñānam*
saṃskāra (m.) (see I:18)

sākṣāt (m. abl. sg.) from the perception of; with one's own eyes; evident to the senses; *sa* (with) + *akṣa* (eye) [end of TP7 cpd.]

karaṇāt (m. abl. sg.) doing, making, effecting; from $\sqrt{kṛ}$ (made, do)

pūrva (ind.) previous (see I:18)

jāti (f.) birth (see II:13)

jñānam (n. nom. sg.) knowledge (see I:18) [end of TP6 cpd.]

From effecting the perception of *saṃskāra*, there is knowledge of previous births.

19. *pratyasya para-citta-jñānam*

pratyayasya (m. gen. sg.) intention (see I:10)

para (m.) another, different from; from $\sqrt{pṛ}$ (rescue, protect)

citta (n.) mind, thought (see I:2) [end of TP7 cpd.]

jñānam (n. nom. sg.) knowledge (see I:8) [end of TP7 cpd.]

[Similarly, from perception of another's] intention, there is knowledge of another mind.

20. *na ca tat sālambanaṃ tasya aviṣayī bhūtatvāt*

na (ind.) not

ca (ind.) and or but

tad (n. nom. sg.) that (see I:12)

sālambanam (m. nom. sg.) with support, with basis; *sa* (with) + *ālambana* (see I:10)

tasya (m. nom. sg.) of it (see (I:27)

aviṣayī (m. nom. sg.) without having an object or condition; *a* (not) + *viṣayin*, from *viṣaya* (condition), see I:11 + *in*, possessive suffix

bhūtatvāt (n. abl. sg.) element, constituent of the manifest world; from *bhūta* (see II:18) + *tva*, suffix denoting "having the quality of"

But this is not with support because there is no condition of it in the elements.

The knowledge residing at the subtle level has no corresponding form in the manifest realm of the elements.

21. *kāya-rūpa-saṃyamāt tad grāhya-śakti-stambhe cakṣuḥ prakā-śa-asaṃyoge antardhānam*

kāya (m.) body (see II:43)

rūpa (n.) form, one of the *tanmātras* (see I:3) [end of TP6 cpd.]

saṃyamāt (m. abl. sg.) from *saṃyama* (see III:4) [end of TP7 cpd.]

tad (n.) that (see I:12)

grāhya (m.) to be grasped (see I:41)

śakti (f.) power (see II:6) [end of TP6 cpd.]

stambhe (m. loc. sg.) suspension, supression, stoppage (see II:50) [end of TP7 cpd.]

cakṣus (m. nom. sg.) eye, from √*cakṣ* (see)

prakāśa (m.) light (see II:18) [end of TP6 cpd.]

asaṃyoge (m. loc. sg.) disjunction, disunion; *a* (not) + *saṃyoga* (union), see II:18; [end of TP6 cpd.] (end of locative absolute construction)

antardhānam (n. nom. sg.) hidden, concealed, invisible; from *antar* (between) + *dhāna*. from √*dhā* (put)

From *saṃyama* on the form (*rūpa*) of the body, [there arises] the suspension of the power of what is to be grasped and the disjunction of light and the eye, resulting in concealment.

Most interpretations have read this *sūtra* as stating that a yogi has the power of invisibility. In understanding how light reflected off a body allows a person to be seen, the yogi is able to avoid being observed. This could refer also to the yogi's ability to suspend the grasping of the world through control over the *tanmātras;* he or she is able to render things hidden or invisible due to his nonactivation of the power of grasping.

22. *sopakramaṃ nirupakramaṃ ca karman tad saṃyamāt aparānta-jñānam ariṣṭebhyaḥvā*

sopakramaṃ (n. nom. sg.) set in motion, undertaken; *sa* (with) + *pa* (to, unto)+ *krama*, from $\sqrt{kram}$ (step)

nirupakramaṃ (n. nom. sg.) not in motion, not taken up, not pursued; *nir* (away from) + *upakrama* (see above)

ca (ind.) and

karman (n. nom. sg.) action (see I:24)

tad (n.) that

saṃyamāt (m. abl. sg.) from *saṃyama* (see III:4) [end of TP7 cpd.]

aparānta (m.) literally, the "Western extremity;" the latter end, conclusion, death

jñānam (n. nom. sg.) knowledge (see I:18)

ariṣṭebhyaḥ (m. abl. pl.) from natural phenomena boding misfortune, ill omens, signs of approaching death; *a* (not) + *riṣṭa*, from $\sqrt{riṣ}$ (be hurt)

va (ind.) or

Karma is either in motion or not in motion. From *saṃyama* on this, or from natural phenomena boding misfortune, there is knowledge of death.

23. *maitrī ādiṣu balāni*

maitrī (f.) friendliness (see I:33)

ādiṣu (m. loc. pl.) and so forth, etc.

balāṇi (n. nom. pl.) powers, strengths; from $\sqrt{bal}$ (breathe, live)

(By *saṃyama*) on friendliness and so forth, (corresponding)

powers.

This appears to be a reference to the Brahma Vihāra (see I:33).

24. *baleṣu hasti-bala-ādīni*
  baleṣu (n. loc. pl.) in powers (see III:23)
  hasti (m.) elephant
  bala (n.) power (see III:23) [end of KD cpd.]
  ādīni (n. nom. pl.) and so forth, etc.

[By *saṃyama*] on powers, the powers like those of the elephant, and so forth.

25. *pravṛtti-āloka-nyāsāt sūkṣma-vyavahita-viprakṛṣṭa-jñānam.*
  pravṛtti (f.) activity (see I:35)
  āloka (m.) light (see III:5) [end of TP7 cpd.]
  nyāsāt (m. abl. sg.) placing down or setting down, applying, casting; *ni* (down, into) + √*ās* (sit) [end of TP6 cpd.]
  sūkṣma (m.) subtle (see I:44)
  vyavahita (m.) concealed, obstructed, *vi* (asunder, away) + *ava* (down) + *hita*, from √*dhā* (place, put)
  viprakṛṣṭa (m.) distant, remote; *vi* (asunder, away) + *pra* (before) + *kṛṣṭa*, from √*kṛṣ* (drag, plough) [end of DV cpd.]
  jñānam (n. nom. sg.) knowledge (see I:8) [end of TP6 cpd.]

Due to the casting of light on a [sense] activity, there is knowledge of the subtle, concealed, and distant.

26. *bhuvana-jñānam sūrye saṃyamāt*
  bhuvana (n.) world, cosmic region; from √*bhū* (be)
  jñānaṃ (n. nom. sg.) knowledge (see I:8) [end of TP6 cpd.]
  surye (m. loc. sg.) on the sun
  saṃyamāt (m. abl. sg.) from *saṃyama* (see III:4)

From *saṃyama* on the sun, [arises] knowledge of the world.

27. *candre tārā-vyūha-jñānam*
   candre (m. loc. sg.) on the moon, from √*cand* (shine)
   tārā (f.) star, from √*tṛ* (pass beyond)
   vyūha (m.) ordering, arrangement, distribution; from *vi* (asunder, away) + √*vūh* (remove)
   jñānam (n. nom. sg.) knowledge (see I:8) [end of TP6 cpd.]

On the moon, knowledge of the ordering of the stars.

28. *dhruve tad gati-jñānam*
   dhruve (m. loc. sg.) on the polar star
   tad (n.) that (refers to stars in prior *sūtra*)
   gati (f.) motion (see II:14)
   jñānam (n. nom. sg.) knowledge (see I:8) [end of TP6 cpd.]

On the polar star, knowledge of their movement.

29. *nābhi-cakre kāya-vyūha-jñānam*
   nābhi (f.) central point, naval
   cakre (n. loc. sg.) a center of energy in the body; wheel, circle; reduplicated derivative of √*kṛ* (do) [end of KD cpd.]
   kāya (m.) body (see II:43)
   vyūha (m.) arrangement (see III:127) [end of TP6 cpd.]
   jñānam (n. nom. sg.) knowledge (see I;8) [end of TP6 cpd.]

On the central *cakra*, knowledge of the ordering of the body.

30. *kaṇṭha-kūpe kṣut-pipāsā-nivṛttiḥ*
   kaṇṭha (m.) throat, neck
   kūpe (m. loc. sg.) hollow, cavity, well [end of TP6 cpd.]
   kṣudh (f.) hunder, from √*kṣudh* (to hunger)
   pipāsā (f.) thirst, wishing to drink; desiderative form of √*pā* (drink) [end of DV cpd.]

nivṛttiḥ (f. nom. sg.) cessation, disappearance; from *ni* (down, into) + *vṛtti* (see I:2) [end of TP6 cpd.]

On the hollow of the throat, cessation of hunger and thirst.

31. *kūrma-nāḍyām sthairyam*

kūrma (m.) tortoise, turtle

nāḍyāṃ (f. loc. sg.) pathway of *prāṇa* (energy); vein or artery [end of KD cpd.]

sthairyam (n. nom. sg.) firmness, stability, steadfastness; from √*sthā* (stand)

On the tortoise *nāḍi*, stability.

32. *mūrdha-jyotiṣi siddha-darśanam*

mūrdha (m.) head

jyotiṣi (n. loc. sg.) light, brightness; from *mūrdha* √*jyut* (shine) [end of TP7 cpd.]

siddha (m.) perfected one, accommplished one, sacred, powerful (see II:43)

darśanam (n. nom. sg.) vision (see I:30) [end of TP6 cpd.]

On the light in the head, vision of perfected ones.

33. *prātibhād vā sarvam*

prātibhād (m. abl. sg.) intuition, vividness; from *pra* (before) + *ati* (over, beyond) + √*bha* (shine)

vā (ind.) or, and

sarvam (n. nom. sg.) all, everything (see I:25)

Or from intuition, everything.

34. *hṛdaye citta-saṃvit*

hṛdaye (n. loc. sg.) heart; the seat of the feelings and sensations

citta (n.) mind (see I:2)
saṃvid (f. nom. sg.) understanding, knowledge; from *sam* (together) + $\sqrt{vid}$ (know)

On the heart, understanding of the mind.

35. *sattva-puruṣayor atyanta-asaṃkīrṇayoḥ pratyaya-aviśeṣaḥ bhogaḥ para-arthatvāt svārtha-saṃyamāt puruṣa-jñānam*
sattva (n.) lightness, beingness (see II:41)
puruṣayor (m. loc. du.) (see I:16) [end of DV cpd.]
atyanta (m.) perfect, endless, unbroken, perpetual, very great; *ati* (over, beyond) + *anta* (end)
asaṃkīrṇayoḥ (m. gen. du.) unmixed, not unclean, not confused, pure, distinct; *a* (not) + *saṃkīrṇa* (see I:42) [end of DV cpd.]
pratyaya (m.) intention (see I:10)
aviśeṣaḥ (m. nom. sg.) indistinct (see II:19) [end of TP6 cpd.]
bhogaḥ (m. nom. sg.) experience (see II:13)
para (m.) other (see III:19)
arthatvāt (m. abl. sg.) due to purpose (see I:49) [end of TP4 cpd.]
svārtha (m. or n.) purpose for the self; *sva* (own) + *artha* (purpose) see I:28
saṃyamāt (m. abl. sg.) from *saṃyama* (see III:4) (end of TP7 cpd.)
puruṣa (m.) (see I:16)
jñānam (n. nom. sg.) knowledge (see I:8) (end of TP6 cpd.)

When there is no distinction of intention between the pure *puruṣa* and the perfect *sattva*, there is experience for the purpose of the other [*puruṣa*]; from *saṃyama* on purpose being for the self, there is knowledge of *puruṣa*.
See *Sāṃkhya Kārikā* 17.

36. *tataḥ prātibha-śrāvaṇa-vedanā-ādarśa-āsvāda-vārtāḥ jāyante*

tataḥ (ind.) hence (see I:22)

prātibha (m.) intuition, vividness (see III:33)

śrāvaṇa (m.) hearing, relating to or perceived by the ear; from √*śru* (hear)

vedanā (f.) touching, feeling, sensing; from √*vid* (know)

ādarśa (m.) seeing, act of perceiving by the eyes; *ā* (hither, unto) + *darśa*, from √*dṛś* (see)

āsvāda (m.) tasting, enjoying, eating; from *ā* (hither, unto) + *svāda*, from √*svad* (eat)

vārtāḥ (m. nom. pl.) smelling [end of five part DV cpd., each member of which is modified by the term *prātibha*, hence forming an extended KD cpd.]

jāyante (third person plural, present middle) are born or produced; from √*jan* (be born)

Hence are born intuitive hearing, touching, seeing, tasting, and smelling.

These five enhanced abilities can observe the subtle elements (*tanmātras*) giving birth to the gross elements. It is clear that Patañjali is closely following Sāṃkhya.

37. *te samādhau upasargāḥ vyutthāne siddhayaḥ*

te (m. nom. pl.) these (see I:30)

samādhau (f. loc. sg.) in *samādhi* (see I:20)

upasargāḥ (m. nom. pl.) impediment, obstacle, trouble; *upa* (to, unto) + *sarga*, from √*sṛj* (create)

vyutthāne (m. loc. sg.) in emergence (see III:9)

siddhayaḥ (f. nom. pl.) perfections (see II:43)

These are impediments to *samādhi*; in emergence (world production), they are perfections.

38. *bandha-kāraṇa-śaithilyāt pracāra-saṃvedanāt ca cittasya*

para-śarīra-āveśaḥ

bandha (m.) binding, holding, bondage (see III:1)

kāraṇa (n.) reason, cause, motive, origin; from √*kṛ* (do)

śaithilyāt (m. abl. sg.) relaxation (see II:47)

pracāra (m.) coming forth, showing oneself, manifestation, appearance; *pra* (before, forward) + *cāra*, from √*car* (move)

saṃvedanāt (n. abl. sg.) the act of perceiving or feeling; perception, sensation; *sam* (together) + *vedana*, from √*vid* (know)

ca (ind.) and

cittasya (n. gen. sg.) of the mind or consciousness (see I:2)

para (m.) other (see III:19)

śarīra (n.) body, that which is subject to decay; from √*śṛ* (crush)

āveśaḥ (m. nom. sg.) entrance, taking possession of, entering; *ā* (hither, unto) + *veśa*, from √*viś* (enter)

From the relaxation of the cause of bondage and from the perception of a manifestation, there is an entering of the mind into another embodiment.

In loosening the bonds of karma, the yogi realizes how karma is assembled and disassembled and there by can move from one assemblage to another. Also, by focusing on perfected beings (as in tantra), those qualities of perfection are embodied (see II:44). Compare this to verses in the *Bhagavad Gītā* where Krishna advises Arjuna to surrender to him, saying the yogin "goes to union with me" (*yogi...matsaṃsthām adhigacchati*) VI:15, an event that takes place in Chapter XI.

39. *udāna-jayāt jala-paṅka-kaṇṭaka-ādiṣu asaṅgaḥ ukrāntiś ca*

udāna (m.) upbreath, one of the five vital breaths; *ud* (up) + *āna*, from √*an* (breathe)

jayāt (m. abl. sg.) from mastery (see II:41) [end of TP6

cpd.]
jala (n.) water
paṅka (m.) mud
kaṇṭaka (m.) thorn
ādiṣu (m. loc. pl.) and so forth, etc. [end of DV cpd.]
asaṅgaḥ (m. nom. sg.) unattached, free from ties, independent; *a* (not) + *saṅga*, from √*sañj* (cling)
utkrāntiḥ (f. nom. sg.) rising, stepping up, passing away, dying; *ud* (up) + *krānti*, from √*kram* (stride)
ca (ind.) and

From mastery of the upbreath, there is nonattachment amongst water, mud, and thorns, etc., and a rising above.

Compare with *Bhagavad Gītā* II:23 "Weapons do not pierce this, fire does not burn this, waters do not wet this, nor does wind dry it."

40. *samāna-jayāt jvalanam*
samāna (m.) breath of the middle region; *sam* (together) + *āna*, from √*an* (breathe)
jayāt (m. abl. sg.) mastery (see II:41) [end of TP6 cpd.]
jvalanam (n. nom. sg.) radiance, effulgence, shining; from √*jval* (burn, flame)

From mastery of the *samāna*, there is radiance.

41. *śrotva-ākāśayoḥ saṃbandha-saṃyamād divyam śrotram*
śrotra (n.) ear; from √*śrū* (hear)
ākaśayoḥ (n. gen. du.) space, ether; *ā* (to, unto) + *kāśa*, from √*kāś* (appear, make a show)
saṃbandha (m.) connection, union, association; *sam* (together) + *bandha*, from √*bandh* (bind)
saṃyamāt (m. abl. sg.) from *saṃyama* (see III:4)

divyam (n. nom. sg.) divine, heavenly, wonderful
śrotram (n. nom. sg.) ear

From *saṃyama* on the connection between the ear and space, [there arises] the divine ear.
The divine ear literally "hears" distance into existence.

The last and most subtle of the gross elements is mastered here.

42. *kāya-ākāśayoḥ saṃbandha-saṃyamāt laghu-tūla-samāpatteḥ ca ākāśa-gamamam*
kāya (m.) body (see II:43)
ākāśayoḥ (n. gen. du.) space (see III:41)
saṃbandha (m.) connection (see III:41)
saṃyamāt (m. abl. sg.) from *saṃyama* (see III:4)
laghu (m.) light, easy, not difficult
tūla (n.) cotton, tuft of grass or reeds
samāpatteḥ (f. abl. sg.) unity (see I:41) [end of TP6 cpd.]
ca (ind.) and
ākāśa (n.) space (see III:41)
gamanam (n. nom. sg.) movement, going; from √*gam* (go) [end of KD cpd.]

From *saṃyama* on the connection between the body and space, and from unity with the lightness of cotton, there is movement through space.
Though meditation on the lightness of cotton, the mind (*citta*), which pervades the whole body, takes on its qualities (see III:38).

43. *bahir akalpitā vṛttir mahā-videhā tataḥ prakāśa-āvaraṇa-kṣayaḥ*
bahir (ind.) outer, external (see III:8)
akalpitā (f. nom. sg.) genuine, not artificial; *a* (not) + *kalpitā*,

from √*kḷp* (be adapted)
vrttiḥ (f. nom. sg.) fluctuation (see I:2)
mahā (m.) great (see II: 31)
videhā (f. nom. sg.) discarnate (see I:19) [end of KD cpd.]
tataḥ (ind.) hence (see I:22)
prakāśa (m.) light (see II:18)
āvaraṇa (n.) covering (see II:18)
kṣayaḥ (m. nom. sg.) destruction; from √*kṣip* (see II:28) [end TP6 cpd.]

An outer, genuine fluctuation is the great discarnate; hence the covering of light is destroyed.
In this state, the yogi experiences bodiless absorption. (See I: 19, as well as II:52 and III:38).)

44. *sthūla-svarūpa-sūkṣma-anvaya-arthavattva-saṃyamād bhūta-jayaḥ*

sthūla (m.) gross, coarse, solid, material; from √*sthā* (stand)
svarūpa (n.) own form (see I:3) [end of TP6 cpd.]
sūkṣma (m.) subtle (see I:44) [end of TP6 cpd.]
anvaya (m.) connection (see III:9)
arthavattva (n.) significance, importance; from *artha* (purpose) + *vat* (suffix indicating possession) + *tva* (suffix indicating "having the quality of") [end of DV cpd.]
saṃyamāt (m. abl. sg.) (see III:4) [end of TP7 cpd.]
bhūta (m.) element (see II:18)
jayaḥ (m. nom. sg.) mastery (see II:41) [end of TP6 cpd.]

From *saṃyama* the own form, on the significance and connection of the subtle and the own form of the gross, there is mastery over the elements.
The arisal of the gross stems from the subtle; by investigating the relationship between the two, mastery over the gross is achieved. See III:47, which links sensing, the approach to the gross, with the

sense of self, which is more subtle.

45. *tataḥ-aṇima-ādi-prādurbhāvaḥ kāya-saṃpat tad-dharma-anabhigātaś ca*

tatas (ind.) hence

aṇima (m.) minuteness, fineness, thinness

ādi (ind.) and so forth, etc.

prādurbhāvaḥ (m. nom. sg.) appearance, that which is visible (see III:9) [end of TP6 cpd.]

kāya (m.) body (see II: 43)

saṃpad (f. nom. sg.) perfection, success, accomplishment, fulfillment; *sam* (together) + √*pad* (go) [end of TP6 cpd.]

tad (n.) that

dharma (m.) (see III:13) [end of TP6 cpd.]

anabhigātaḥ (m. nom. sg.) unassailability (see II:48) [end of TP6 cpd.]

ca (ind.) and

Hence arise the appearance of minuteness and so forth, perfection of the body, and unassailability of its *dharma*.

Perfection of the body does not arise in regard to a standard of health, but proceeds from a comprehension of the operation of the *tattvas*. See *Bhagavad Gtā* XIII: 2-5.

Also, "unassailability of its *dharma*" refers to the yogi's ability to maintain a particular embodiment without the normal limits imposed by his experience of the elements.

46. *rūpa-lāvaṇya-bala-vajra-saṃhananatvāni kāya-saṃpat*

rūpa (n.) form (see I:8)

lāvaṇya (n.) beauty, loveliness [end of TP6 cpd.]

bala (n.) strength, power, might, vigor; from √*bal* (breathe, live)

vajra (m.) thunderbolt; hard, mighty, adamantine; from √*vaj* (be strong)

saṃhananatvāni (n. nom. pl.) solidity, robustness, firmness, steadfastness; *sam* (together) + *hanana*, from $\sqrt{han}$ (strike) + *tva*, suffix denoting "having the quality of" [end of DV cpd.]
kāya (m.) body (see II:43)
saṃpad (f. nom. sg.) perfection (see III:45) [end of TP6 cpd.]

Perfection of the body is beauty of form, strength, and adamantine stability.

47. *grahaṇa-svarūpa-asmitā-anvaya-arthavattva-saṃyamād indriya-jayaḥ*
grahaṇa (m.) grasping (see I:41)
svarūpa (n.) own-form (see I:3)
asmitā (f.) I-am-ness (see I:17)
anvaya (m.) connection (see: III:9)
arthavattva (n.) significance (see III:44)
indriya (n.) sense organ (see II:18)
jayaḥ (m. nom. sg.) mastery (see II:41) [end of TP6 cpd.]

From *saṃyama* on grasping, own form, I-am-ness, their connection, and their significance, there is mastery over the sense organs.
This parallels III:44 above. In the earlier *sūtra*, the gross is linked to the elements, In this *sūtra*, the subtle sense of I-am-ness is linked to the sense organs.

48. *tato mano-javitvaṃ vikaraṇa-bhāvaḥ pradhāna-jayaś ca*
tataḥ (ind.) hence (see I:22)
manas (n.) mind organ (see I:35)
javitvaṁ (n. nom. sg.) swiftness, speed; from $\sqrt{jā}$ (be born)
vikaraṇa (m.) deprived of organs of sense; *vi* (asunder, away) + *karaṇa* (organ of sense), from $\sqrt{kṛ}$ (do)
bhāvaḥ (m. nom. sg.) state of becoming, being, existing; true state or condition; temperament, nature; way of thinking,

disposition; from $\sqrt{}$*bhū* (be) [end of KD cpd.]

pradhāna (n.) originator, original source of the manifest; *prakṛti; pra* (before, forward) + *dhāna*, from $\sqrt{}$*dhā* (put)

jayaḥ (m. nom. sg.) mastery (see II: 41) [end of TP6 cpd.]

ca (ind.) and

Hence, there is swiftness of the mind organ, a state of being beyond the senses, and mastery over the *pradhāna*.

49. *sattva-puruṣa-anyatā-khyāti-mātrasya sarva-bhāva-adhiṣṭhātṛtvaṃ sarva-jñātṛtvaṃ ca*

sattva (n.) (see II:41)

puruṣa (m.) (see I:16) [end of DV cpd.]

anyatā (f.) difference, distinction; *anya* (other) + *tā* (feminine suffix denoting "having the power of") [end of TP6 cpd.]

khyāti (f.) discernment (see I:16) [end of TP6 cpd.]

mātrasya (m. gen. sg.) only (see I: 43) [end of BV cpd.]

sarva (n.) all (see I:25)

bhāva (m.) state of being (see III:48)

adhiṣṭhātṛtvaṃ (n. nom. sg.) sovereignty, rulership, supremacy; *adhi* (over, on) + *ṣṭhātṛ*, stander, from $\sqrt{}$*sthā* (stand) + *tṛ* (agentive suffix) + *tvam* (neuter suffix denoting "having the quality of")

sarva (n.) all (see I:25)

jñātṛtvaṃ (n. nom. sg.) knowledge; literally, the quality stemming from being a knower; $\sqrt{}$*jñā* (know) + *tṛ* (agentive suffix) + *tvam* (see above)

ca (ind.) and

Only from the discernment of the difference between *sattva* and *puruṣa*, there is sovereignty over all states of being and knowledge of all.

At the most subtle of levels, the distinction is seen between the finest aspect of *prakṛti* and the inactive *puruṣa*. From this ability proceeds supreme knowledge and power.

50. *tad-vairāgyād api doṣa-bīja-kṣaye kaivalyaṃ*

tad (n.) this

vairāgyāt (n. abl. sg.) dispassion (see I:12) [end of TP4 cpd.]

api (ind.) even (see I:22)

doṣa (m.) impediment, deteriment, fault, want; from √*duṣ* (spoil)

bīja (n.) seed (see I:25)

kṣaye (m. loc. sg.) destruction (see II:28) [end of TP6 cpd.]

kaivalyaṃ (m. loc. sg.) isolation (see II:25)

From dispassion toward even this, in the destruction of the seed of this impediment, arises *kaivalyam*.

51. *sthāny-upanimantraṇe saṅga-smaya-akaraṇaṃ punar aniṣṭa-prasaṅgāt*

sthāni (m.) well-estalished, having a place, being in the right place; original form; from √*sthā* (stand) + *in* (possessive suffix)

upanimantraṇe (n. loc. sg.) invitation, offer; from *upa* (to, unto) + *mantraṇa* (consultation), from *mantra* (sacred speech), from √*man* (think) [end of TP5 cpd.]

saṅga (m.) attachment (see III:39)

smaya (m.) pride, arrogance; smiling; from √*smi* (smile) [end of DV cpd.]

akaraṇam (n. nom. sg.) no cause (see III:38)

punar (ind.) again (see III:12)

aniṣṭa (m.) unwanted, undesirable; *an* (not) + *iṣṭa*, from √*iṣ* (wish)

prasaṅgāt (m. abl. sg.) association, devotion to, attachment, adherence; from *pra* (before, forward) + *saṅga*, from √*sañj* (cling)

There is no cause for attachment and pride upon the invitation of those well established, because of repeated association with the undesirable.

Even if one is tempted to re-enter the realm of attachment, the momentum to do so has ceased, because one is constantly aware of the undesirable outcome of such a return. See I:15.

52. ***kṣaṇa-tat-kramayoḥ samyamād viveka-jaṃ jñ ānaṃ***

kṣaṇa (n.) moment (see III:9)
tad (n.) this
kramayoḥ (m. loc. du.) successsion (see III:15) [end of DV cpd.]
saṃyamāt (m. abl. sg.) (see III:4)
viveka (m.) discrimination (see II:15)
jaṃ (n. nom. sg.) born of (see I:50) [end of TP5 cpd.]
jñ ānaṃ (n. nom. sg.) knowledge (see I:8)

From *saṃyama* on the moment and its succession, there is knowledge born of discrimination.

53. *jāti-lakṣaṇa-deśair anyatā anavacchedāt tulyayoḥ taṭaḥ pratipattiḥ*

jāti (f.) birth (see II:13)
lakṣaṇa (m.) designation (see III:13)
deśair (m. instr. pl.) place (see II:31) [end of DV cpd.]
anyatā (f. nom. sg.) difference (see III:49)
anavacchedāt (m. abl. sg.) unlimited, not separated (see I:26)
tulyayoḥ (m. gen. du.) sameness (see III:12)
tataḥ (ind.) hence (see I:22)
pratipattiḥ (f. nom. sg.) perception, observation, ascertainment, acknowledgement; from *prati* (against, back) + *patti*, from $\sqrt{}$*pad* (go)

Hence, there is the ascertainment of two things that are similar, due to their not being limited (made separate) by differences of birth, designation, and place.

The traditional reading of Vyāsa states that a yogī is able to tell two identical items apart despite their occupying the same space but at different times. This signifies that all things are in a state of flux.

As a variant reading, this *sūtra* might refer to the similarity between the *sattva* or unmanifest form of *prakṛti* and the *puruṣa*. For a list of their similarities, see *Sāṃkhya Kārikā* XI. The key to liberation is to be able to see the difference between these two; this is the highest *siddhi* of *kaivalyam*. This interpretation is borne out by the context before and after this passage. (See III:49 and III:55.)

54. *tārkam sarva-viṣayaṃ sarvathā viṣayaṃ akramaṃ ca iti viveka-jaṃ jñānaṃ*

tārakam (n. nom. sg.) enabling one to cross over; rescuing, liberating, saving; from *tāra*, protector, from $\sqrt{t\d{r}}$ (pass)
sarva (n.) all (see I:25)
viṣayam (n. nom. sg.) condition (see I:11) [end of BV cpd.]
sarvathā (ind.) in every way or respect; at all times; from *sarva* (all) + *thā* (temporal suffix)
viṣayaṃ (n. nom. sg.) object (see I:11)
akramaṃ (n. nom. sg.) nonsuccessive (see III:15)
ca (ind.) and
iti (ind.) thus
vivekā (m.) discrimination (see II:15)
jaṃ (n. nom. sg.) born of (see I:50) [end of TP5 cpd.]
jñānaṃ (n. nom. sg.) knowledge (see I:8)

The knowledge born of discrimination is said to be liberating, (inclusive of) all conditions and all times, and nonsuccessive.

55. *sattva-puruṣayoḥ śuddhi-sāmye kaivalyaṃ iti*

sattva (n.) (see II:41)
puruṣayoḥ (m. gen. du.) (see I:16) [end of DV cpd.]
śuddhi (f.) purity (see II:28)

sāmye (n. loc. sg.) evenness, sameness; from *sama* (same) [end of TP6 cpd.]

kaivalyaṃ (n. nom. sg.) isolation (see II:25)

iti (ind.) thus

In the sameness of purity between the *sattva* and the *puruṣa*, there is *kaivalyam*.

IV: *Kaivalya-pāda*

1. *janma-oṣadhi-mantra-tapaḥ-samādhi-jāḥ siddayaḥ*
   janma (n.) birth, existence (see II:12)
   oṣadhi (f.) medicinal herb, remedy, drug
   mantra (m.) sacred formula or speech, prayer, song of praise, mystical verse; from $\sqrt{}$*man* (think)
   tapaḥ (n.) austerity (see (II:1)
   samādhi (f.) absorption (see I:20) [end of DV cpd.]
   jāḥ (m. nom. pl.) born (see I:50) [end of TP5 cpd.]
   siddhayaḥ (f. nom. pl.) perfection (see II:43)

Perfections are born due to birth, drugs, *mantra*, austerity, or *samādhi*.

2. *jāti-antara-pariṇāmaḥ prakṛty-āpūrāt*
   jāti (f.) birth (see II:13)
   antara (m.) different, other, another [end of TP6 cpd.]
   pariṇāmaḥ (m. nom. sg.) (see II:15) [end of TP7 cpd.]
   prakṛti (f.) (see I:19)
   āpūrāt (m. abl. sg.) excess, abundance, flooding; *ā* (to, unto) + *pūra*, from $\sqrt{}$*pṛ* (fill) [end of TP6 cpd.]

From the flooding of *prakṛti*, arises *pariṇāma* into other births. Whatever *saṃskāras* remain cause future experiences to unfold.

3. *nimittam aprayokakaṃ prakṛtīnāṃ varaṇa-bhedas tu tataḥ kṣetrikavat*
   nimittaṃ (n. nom. sg.) cause, motive, ground, reason; instrumental cause; *ni* (down, into) + *mitta*, from $\sqrt{}$*mā* (measure)
   aprayokakaṃ (n. nom. sg.) not causing or effecting; not initiating, prompting or instigating; *a* (not) + *pra* (before) +

yojaka, from √*yuj* (join)
prakṛtīnāṃ (f. gen. pl.) manifestations (see I:9)
varaṇa (n.) surrounding, enclosing so as to limit; from √*vṛ* (cover)
bhedaḥ (m. nom. sg.) separation, division, distinction; from √*bhid* (split) (end of BV cpd.)
tu (ind.) but
tataḥ (ind.) hence
kṣetrikavat (m. nom. sg.) like a farmer; like the owner of a field; *kṣetra* (field) + *ika* (possessive suffix) + *vat* (suffix indicating likeness)

Hence, [those things that] make distinct the limitations of these manifestations are the instrumental cause, not the initiator, as in the case of the farmer (who does not initiate the flow of water put directs it through the use of barriers).
The pathways of manifestations are determined by *saṃskāras* alrendy in motion. This *sūtra* explains how the flooding of *prakṛti* mentioned above takes it course.

4. *nirmāṇa-cittāni asmitā-mātrāt*
nirmāṇa (m.) creating, making, forming, fabricating; *nir* (out, away from) + *māna*, from √*mā* (measure)
cittāni (n. nom. pl.) mind (see I:2) [end of KD cpd.]
asmitā (f.) I-am-ness (see I:17, II:3, II:6)
mātrāt (m. abl. sg.) only (see I:43) [end of KD cpd.]

The fabricating minds arise only from I-am-ness.

5. *pravṛtti-bhede prayojakaṃ cittaṃ ekaṃ anekeṣāṃ*
pravṛtti (f.) activity (see I:35)
bhede (m. loc. sg.) distinction (see (IV:3) [end of TP5 cpd.]
prayojakaṃ (n. nom. sg.) initiator (see IV:3)
cittam (n. nom. sg.) mind (see I:2)
ekam (n. nom. sg.) one (see I:26)

anekesām (n. gen. pl.) many; *an* (not) + *eka* (one)

The initiator is the one mind among many that is distinct from activity.

This most probably would be the intellect in its most subtle form of *sattva*, which we saw earlier (III:55) as associated with *kaivalyam*. All mind is in some sense active, but this "one mind" is like *puruṣa* and hence pure. The following verse seems to confirm this position.

6. *tatra dhyāna-jaṃ anāśayaṃ*
   tatra (ind.) there (see I:13)
   dhyāna (m.) meditation (see I:39)
   jaṃ (n. nom. sg.) born (see I:50) (end of TP5 cpd.)
   anāśayaṃ (n. nom. sg.) without residue; *an* (not) + *āśaya* (residue), see I:24

There, what is born of meditation is without residue.

7. *karma-aśukla-akṛṣṇaṃ yoginas trividhaṃ itaresāṃ*
   karma (m. nom. sg.) action (see I:24)
   aśukla (n.) not white; *a* (not) + *śukla* (white, pure, stainless), from $\sqrt{}$*śuc* (gleam)
   akṛṣnaṃ (n. nom. sg.) not black; *a* (not) + *kṛṣṇa* (black, dark)
   yoginas (m. gen. sg.) yogin, one who has yoga; *yoga* (see I:1) + *in*, possessive suffix
   trividhaṃ (n. nom. sg.) threefold; *tri* (three) + *vidha* (division, part), from *vi* (asunder, away) + *dha*, from $\sqrt{}$*dhā* (put)
   itaresāṃ (m gen. pl.) others (see I:20)

The action of a yogin is neither white nor black; that of others is threefold.

(Black, white, and mixed.)

8. *tatas tad-vipāka-anuguṇānām eva abhivyaktir vāsanānāṃ*

tatas (ind.) hence (see I:22)

tad (n.) that

vipāka (m.) fruition (see I:24)

anuguṇānāṃ (m. gen. pl.) having similar qualities; *anu* (along, after) + *guṇa* (see I:16)

eva (ind.) thus, only (see I:44)

abhivyaktir (f. nom. sg.) manifestation, distinction; *abhi* (to, unto) + *vyakti*, from *vi* (asunder, away) + *akti*, from $\sqrt{}$*añj* (annoint)

vāsanānāṃ (f. gen. pl.) habit pattern; impression of anything remaining unconsciously in the mind; inclination; from $\sqrt{}$*vas* (dwell)

Hence, the manifestation of habit patterns thus corresponds to the fruition of that (*karma*).

This *sūtra* states that action one performs proceeds according to the residue of past action (*saṃskāra* or *vāsanā*).

9. *jāti-deśa-kāla-vyavahitānāṃ apy ānantaryaṃ smṛti-saṃskārayor eka rūpatvat*

jāti (f.) life state, birth (see II:13)

deśa (m.) place (see II:31)

kāla (m.) time (see I:14) [end of DV cpd.]

vyavahitānāṃ (m. gen. pl.) concealed (see III:25) [end of KD cpd.]

api (ind.) though, even

ānantaryam (n. nom. sg.) link, immediate sequence or succession; from *an* (not) + *antara* (different, see IV:2)

smṛti (f.) memory (see I:16)

saṃskārayor (m. gen. du.) (see I:18) [end of DV cpd.]

eka (n.) one (see I:32)

rūpatvāt (n. nom. sg.) form-ness; *rūpa* (form, see I:3) + *tva* (suffix denoting possession of quality)

Because memory and *saṃskāra* are of one form, there is a link even among births, places, and times that are concealed.
Past actions, even if not remembered, continue to affect present actions.

10. *tāsāṃ anāditvaṃ ca āśiso nityatvāt*

tāsām (m. gen. pl.) of these
anāditvaṃ (n. nom. sg.) state of having no beginning; *an* (not) + *ādi* (and so forth) + *tvam* (suffix denoting quality possessed)
ca (ind.) and
āśisaḥ (f. gen. sg.) asking for, prayer, wish, desire; *ā* (hither, unto) + *śis*, from $\sqrt{}$*śās* (order)
nityatvāt (m. abl. sg.) perpetuity, continuance; *nitya* (eternal, see II:5) + *tva* (see above)

And there is no beginning of these due to the perpetuity of desire.

11. *hetu-phala-āśraya-ālambanaiḥ samgṛhītatvād esāṃ abhāve tad abhāvaḥ*

hetu (m.) cause (see II:17)
phala (n.) fruit (see II:14)
āśraya (n.) correspondence (see II:36)
ālambanaiḥ (m. instr. pl.) based on, supporting (see I:10) [end of DV cpd.]
samgṛhītatvāt (m. abl. sg.) that which is grasped, seized, caught, gathered; *sam* (together) + *gṛhīta*, from $\sqrt{}$*grabh* (grasp) + *tva* (suffix indicating possession of a quality)
eṣāṃ (m. gen. pl.) of these
abhāve (m. loc. sg.) non-becoming (see I:10)
tad (n.) that
abhāvaḥ (m. nom. sg.) non-becoming (see I:10) [end of TP6 cpd.]

Because they are held together by causes, results, correspondences, and supports, when these (go into) nonbeing, (there is the) nonbeing of them (*saṃskāras*).

12. *atīta-anāgataṃ svarūpato asty adhva-bhedād dharmāṇām*

atīta (m.) past (see III:16)

anāgataṃ(n. nom. sg.) yet to come, future (see II:16) [end of DV cpd.]

svarūpataḥ (ind.) in reality, from own form, according to own form; *svarūpa* (see I:3) + *tas* (indeclinable ablative suffix)

asti (pres. ind. 3rd pers. sg.) exists, is; from $\sqrt{as}$ (be)

adhva (m.) path, road, way, course

bhedhāt (m. abl. sg.) distinction (see IV:3) [end of TP6 cpd.]

dharmāṇām (m. gen. pl.) (see III:13)

In their own form, the past and future exist, due to distinctions between paths of *dharmas*.

13. *te vyakta-sūkṣmāḥ guṇa-ātmānaḥ*

te (m. nom. pl.) these

vyakta (n.) manifest, apparent, visible, developed, evolved; *vi* (asunder, away) + *akta* from $\sqrt{a\tilde{n}j}$ (annoint)

sūkṣmāḥ (m. nom. pl.) subtle (see I:44) [end of DV cpd.]

guṇa (m.) (see I:16)

ātmānaḥ (m. nom. pl.) nature (see II:21 and II:5) [end of TP6 cpd.]

These have manifest and subtle *guṇa* natures.

14. *pariṇāma-ekatvād vastu-tattvaṃ*

pariṇāma (m.) (see II:15)

ekatvāt (m. abl. sg.) oneness, uniformity; *eka* (one) + *tva*, suffix denoting "having the quality of" [end of TP6 cpd.]

vastu (n.) object (see I:9)
tattvam (n. nom. sg.) thatness, essence (see I:32) [end of TP6 cpd.]

From the uniformity of its *pariṇāma*, there is the "thatness" of an object.

15. *vastu-sāmye citta-bhedāt tayor vibhaktaḥ panthāḥ*
vastu (n.) object (see I:9)
sāmye (n. loc. sg.) equality (see III:55) [end of TP4 cpd.]
citta (n.) mind (see I:2)
bhedāt (m. abl. sg.) distinction (see IV:3) [end of TP6 cpd.]
tayoḥ (m. gen. du.) of both, each
vibhaktaḥ (m. nom. sg.) divided, distributed, separate; *vi* (asunder, away) + *bhakta*, from √*bhaj* (divide)
panthāḥ (m. nom. sg.) path, way, road, course; from √*path* (go, move)

In the sameness of an object, because of its distinctness from the mind, there is a separate path of each.

16. *na ca eka-citta-tantraṃ vastu tad-apramāṇakaṃ tadā kiṃ syāt*
na (ind.) not
ca (ind.) and
eka (m.) one
citta (n.) mind (see I:2)
tantraṃ (n. nom. sg.) thread, essential part, main point, teaching; from √*tan* (extend)
vastu (n. nom. sg.) object (see I:9)
tad (ind.) that
apramāṇakaṃ (n. nom. sg.) not provable, not demonstrated; *a* (not) + *pra* (before) + *māṇaka*, from √*mā* (measure)
tadā (ind.) then
kiṃ (n. nom. sg.) interrogative pronoun

syāt (3rd pers. optative sg.) could be, from √*as* (be)

An object does not depend on one mind; there is no proof of this: how could it be ?

All objects are made of the *guṇas* of *prakṛti* and are not the product of a single mind. See IV:14.

17. *tad-uparāga-apekṣitvāc cittasya vastu jñāna-ajñātaṃ*

tad (n.) that

uparāga (m.) coloring, dyeing, darkening; influence; *upa* (to) + *rāga*, from √*rañj* (color) [end of TP6 cpd.]

apekṣitvāt (m. abl. sg.) anticipation, expectation; wished, looked for; *apa* (away) + *īkṣitva*, from √*īkṣ* (see) + *tva*, suffix denoting possession of a quality [end of KD cpd.]

cittasya (n. gen. sg.) mind (see I:2)

vastu (n. nom. sg.) object (see I:9)

jñāta (n.) known; from √*jñā* (know)

ajñātaṃ (n. nom. sg.) not known (see above) [end of DV cpd.]

An object of the mind is known or not known due to the anticipation that colors it (the mind).

An object is known only when it colors the mind. This is not realism because there is a coloring of the object by karma. A *pure* object is not known through cognition.

18. *sadā jñātāś citta-vṛttayas tat-prabhoḥ puruṣasya apariṇāmitvāt*

sadā (ind.) always; *sa* (with) + *dā* (temporal indicator)

jñātāḥ (m. nom. pl.) known (see IV:17)

citta (n.) mind (see I:2)

vṛttayas (f. nom. pl.) fluctuations (see I:2)

tad (n.) that

prabhoḥ (m. gen. sg.) master (see I:16)

apariṇāmitvāt (m. abl. sg.) nontransformative, not changing; *a* (not) + *pariṇāma* (see II:15) + *tva*, suffix denoting possession of a quality

The fluctuations of the mind are always known due to the changelessness of their master, *puruṣa*.
See *Sāṃkhya Kārikā* 17 for the proofs establishing *puruṣa*.

19. *na tat-svābhāsaṃ dṛśyatvāt*
na (ind.) not
tad (n.) that
svābhāsaṃ (n. nom. sg.) self luminosity, own light; *sva* (self) + *ābhāsa*, from *ā* (to) + *bhāsa*, from √*bhās* (shine)
dṛśyatvāt (m. abl. sg.) nature of the seen; *dṛśya* (see II:17) + *tva*, suffix denoting possession of quality

There is no self-luminosity of that (*citta-vṛtti*) because of the nature of the seen.
The seen is nonconscious. See *Sāṃkhya Kārikā* 20.

20. *eka-samaye ca ubhaya-anavadhāraṇaṃ*
eka (m.) one (see I:32)
samaye (m. loc. sg.) circumstance (see II:31)
ca (ind.) and
ubhaya (m.) both
anavadhāraṇaṃ (n. nom. sg.) nondiscernment, not ascertaining; *an* (not) + *ava* (down) + *dhāraṇa*, from √*dhṛ* (hold) [end of TP6 cpd.]

In one circumstance, there is no ascertainment of both (*vṛtti* and *puruṣa* together).
The *puruṣa* always remains distinct from circumstance (*prakṛti*).

21. *citta-antara-dṛśye buddhi-buddher atiprasaṅgaḥ smṛti-saṃkaraś ca*

citta (n.) mind (see I:2)
antara (m.) other (see IV:2) [end of KD cpd.]
dṛśye (m. loc. sg.) seen (see II:17) [end of TP6 cpd.]
buddhi (f.) intellect; in Sāṃkhya, the first *tattva* to emerge from *prakṛti*; from √*budh* (awaken)
buddheḥ (f. gen. sg.) intellect (see above) [end of TP5 cpd.]
atiprasaṅgaḥ (m. nom. sg.) excessive attachment, unwarranted stretch of a rule; *ati* (beyond) + *pra* (before) + *saṅga*, from √*sañj* (adhere)
smṛti (f.) memory (see I:6)
saṃkaraḥ (m. nom. sg.) confusion (see III:17) [end of DV cpd.]
ca (ind.) and

In trying to see another higher mind there is an overstretching of the intellect from the intellect and a confusion of memory. Reflecting on the existential implications of this *sūtra*, it seems that this is a warning against trying to get behind your "Self," that is, against trying to find the truly "spiritual" identity which according to this system is impossible: there is no one there to find; the witness cannot be witnessed. See *Bṛhadāraṇyaka Upanisad* III:7:23.

22. *citer apratisaṃkramāyās tad-ākāra-āpattau svabuddhi-saṃvedanam*
citeh (m. gen. sg.) higher awareness; from √*cit* (think)
apratisaṃkramāyāḥ (f. abl. sg.) no intermixture, nondissolution, nonreabsorption; *a* (not) + *prati* (against) + *sam* (together) + *krama*, from √*kram* (step)
tad (n.) that
ākāra (m.) form, figure, shape, appearance; *ā* (hither, unto) + *kāra*, from √*kṛ* (do)
āpattau (f. loc. sg.) happening, occurence, arising, entering into a state or condition; *ā* (hither, unto) + *patti*, from √*pat* (fall, fly) [end of TP6 cpd.]

svabuddhi (f.) own intellect; *sva* (own) + *buddhi* (see IV:21)
saṃvedanam (n. nom. sg.) perception (see III:38) [end of TP6 cpd.]

Due to the nonmixing of higher awareness, entering into that form is [in fact] the perception of one's own intellect.

23. *draṣṭṛ-dṛśya-uparaktaṃ cittaṃ sarva-arthaṃ*
draṣṭṛ (m.) seer (see I:3)
dṛśya (m.) seen (see II:7) (end of DV cpd.)
uparkataṃ (n. nom. sg.) tinted, colored, dyed; *upa* (to, unto) + *rakta*, from √*rañj* (color) (end of TP3 cpd.)
cittaṃ (n. nom. sg.) mind (see I:2)
sarva (n.) all (see I:25)
arthaṃ (n. nom. sg.) meaning, purpose (see I:28) (end of KD cpd.)

All purposes [are known due to] the mind being tinted with seer and seen.
The purpose of all things is to provide experience and liberation, the former through the joining of the seer and seen, the latter through their distinction. See II:18.

24. *tad-asaṃkhyeya-vāsanābhiś-citraṃ api para-arthaṃ saṃhatya kāritvāt*
tad (n.) that
asaṃkhyeya (m.) innumerable, countless, multitude; *a* (not) + *saṃkhyeya*, gerundive form of *saṃkhyā*, *sam* (together) + √*khyā* (see)
vāsanābhiḥ (f. instr. pl.) habit pattern (see IV:8) [end of TP3 cpd.]
citraṃ (n. nom. sg.) variegated, spotted, speckled; various, manifold; from √*cit* (perceive)
api (ind.) also

para (m.) other (see II:40)
arthaṃ (n. nom. sg.) purpose (see I:28) [end of TP6 cpd.]
saṃhatya (ind.) having stuck or put together, joined, combined; gerund form of *sam* (together) + *uhati*, from √*han* (strike)

kāritvāt (n. abl. sg.) action, activity; *kāri*, from √*kṛ* (do) + *tva*, suffix denoting possession of a quality

From action having been done conjointly for the purpose of another, it is speckled with innumerable habit patterns.

Compare with the statement in *Sāṃkhya Kārikā* 36 and 37 that all *prakṛti's* activity is done for the sake of *puruṣa*. See also *Yoga Sūtra* III:35 and IV34.

25. *viśeṣa-darśina ātma-bhāva-bhāvanā-vinivṛttiḥ*

viśeṣa (m.) distinction (see I:22)

darśinaḥ(m. gen. sg.) seer; one who has sight; *darśa*, from √*dṛś* (see) + *in* (possessive suffix) [end of TP6 cpd.]

ātma (m.) self (see II:5)

bhāva (m.) state of being, becoming, existing; condition; intention (see III:9) [end of KD cpd.]

vinivṛttiḥ (f. nom. sg.) turned back, withdrawn, abandoned; cessation, coming to an end, discontinuance; *vi* (asunder, away) + *ni* (down, into) + *vṛtti*, from √*vṛt* (turn) [end of TP6 cpd.]

The one who sees the distinction discontinues the cultivation of self-becoming.

26. *tadā viveka-nimnaṃ kaivalya-prāgbhāraṃ cittaṃ*

tadā (ind.) then

viveka (m.) discrimination (see II:15)

nimnaṃ (n. nom. sg.) inclined towards; bending into; from *ni* (down, into) + *na*, from √*nam* (bend [end of TP7 cpd.]

kaivalya (n.) isolation (see II:25)

prāgbhāraṃ (n. nom. sg.) propensity, inclination, being not far from; from *prāk* (directed towards) + *bhāra*, from √*bhṛ* (bear)
cittaṃ (n.) mind (see I:2)

Then, inclined toward discrimination, the mind has a propensity for *kaivalyaṃ*.

27. *tac-chidreṣu pratyaya-antarāṇi saṃskārebhyaḥ*
tad (n.) that
chidreṣu (m. loc. pl.) torn asunder, containing holes, pierced; defect, fault; from √*chid* (cut)
pratyaya (m.) intention (see I:10)
antarāṇi (n. nom. pl.) other (see IV:2)
saṃskārebhyaḥ (m. abl. pl.) from *saṃskāras* (see I:18)

In the intervening spaces of that, there are other intentions, due to *saṃskāras*.

28. *hānaṃ esāṃ kleśavad uktaṃ.*
hānaṃ (n. nom. sg.) cessation, relinquishment (see II:25)
esāṃ (n. gen. pl.) of those
kleśavat (ind.) like affliction; *kleśa* (see I:24) + *vat* (suffix indicating analogy)
uktaṃ (n. nom. sg.) spoken; past passive participle of √*vac* (speak)

The cessation of them is said to be like that of the afflictions. This process is described in II:10 and II:11 as *pratiprasava* or subtilization.

29. *prasaṃkhyāne'pi akusīdasya sarvathā viveka-khyāter dharma-meghaḥ samādhiḥ*
prasaṃkhyāne (m. loc. sg.) payment, liquidation; (n. loc. sg.) enumeration; reflection, meditation; *pra* (before, forward) +

sam (together) + *khyāna*, from $\sqrt{khyā}$ (see)
api (ind.) also, even, indeed
akusīdasya (m. nom. sg.) taking no interest, without gain, without usury; *a* (not) + *kusīda* (load to be repaid with interest)
sarvathā (ind.) at all times, always (see III:54)
viveka (m.) discrimination (see II:26)
khyāteh (m. gen. sg.) discernment (see I:16) [end of BV cpd.]
dharma (m.) (see III:13)
meghaḥ (m. nom. sg.) cloud; from $\sqrt{mih}$ (sprinkle) [end of KD cpd.]
saṃādhiḥ (f. nom. sg.) absorption (see I:20)

Indeed, in [that state of] reflection, for the one who has discriminative discernment and always takes no interest, there is the cloud of *dharma samādhi*.

An interesting double entendre occurs here; the term *prasaṃkhyāne* can be interpreted either as reflection or as payment. In the latter sense, a financial analogy is used to describe the balancing of the karmic accounts. Once the debts accrued due to past action have been paid off, and no interest remains, then one becomes established in the state of *samādhi* that allows all things to proceed as seen through the liberating knowledge of discriminative discernment.

30. *tataḥ kleśa-karma-nivṛttiḥ*
tataḥ (ind.) from that, thence (see I:22)
kleśa (m.) affliction (see I:24)
karma (n.) action (see I:24) [end of KD cpd.]
nivṛttiḥ (f. nom. sg.) cessation (see III:30) [end of TP6 cpd.]

From that, there is the cessation of afflicted action.

31. *tadā sarva-āvaraṇa-mala-apetasya jñānasya ānantyāj jñeyaṃ alpam*

tadā (ind.) then
sarva (n.) all (see I:25)
āvaraṇa (n.) covering (see II:52)
mala (n.) impurity, dirt, filth, dust
apetasya (m. gen. sg.) departed, gone, departed; free from; *apa* (away, off) + *ita*, from √*i* (go)
jñ*ānasya* (n. gen. sg.) knowledge (see I:8)
ānantyāt (m. abl. sg.) infinite, eternal; from *ananta* (see II:34)
jñeyaṃ (n. nom. sg.) to be known; gerundive form of *jñā* (know)
alpaṃ (n. nom. sg.) little, small

Then, little is to be known due to the eternality of knowledge which is free from all impure covering.

32. *tataḥ kṛta-arthānāṃ pariṇāma-krama-samāptir guṇānāṃ*

tataḥ (ind.) from that, thence (see I:22)
kṛta (m. done (see II:22)
arthānāṃ (n. nom. sg.) purpose (see I:22) [end of KD cpd.]
pariṇāma (m.) (see II:15)
krama (m.) succession (see III:15) [end of TP6 cpd.]
samāptiḥ (f. nom. sg.) conclusion, completion, accomplishment; *sam* (together) + *āpti*, from √*āp* (obtain) [end of TP6 cpd.]
guṇānāṃ (m.) (see I:16)

From that, the purpose of the *guṇas* is done and the succession of *pariṇāma* is concluded.

33. *kṣaṇa-pratiyogī pariṇāma-aparānta-nigrāhyaḥ kramaḥ*

kṣana (n.) moment (see III:9)
pratiyogī (m. nom. sg.) correlate, counterpart, match; *prati*

(against, back) + *yogin*, from $\sqrt{yuj}$ (join) [end of KD cpd.]

pariṇāma (m.) (see II:15)

aparānta (m.) end (see III:22) [end of TP6 cpd.]

nigrāhyaḥ (m. nom. sg.) terminated, to be suppressed; *ni* (down, into) + *grāhya*, gerundive form of $\sqrt{grabh}$ (grasp) [end of TP3 cpd.]

kramaḥ (m. nom. sg.) succession (see III:15)

Succession and its correlate, the moment, are terminated by the end of *pariṇāma*.

34. *puruṣa-artha-śūnyānāṃ guṇānāṃ pratiprasavaḥ kaivalyaṃ svarūpa-pratiṣṭhā vā citi-śaktir iti*

puruṣa (m.) (see I:16)

artha (m.) purpose (see I:28) [end of TP4 cpd.]

śunyānāṃ (m. gen. pl.) empty (see I:9) [end of TP6 cpd.]

guṇānām (m. gen. pl.) (see I:16)

pratiprasavaḥ (m. nom. sg.) return to the origin (see II:10)

kaivalyaṃ (n. nom. sg.) isolation (see II:25)

svarūpa (n.) own form (see I:3)

pratiṣṭhā (f. nom. sg.) steadfastness, perseverence; pre-eminence; *prati* (against, back) + $\sqrt{sth\bar{a}}$ (stand) [end of TP7 cpd.]

va (ind.) or, and

citi (m.) higher awareness (see IV:22)

śaktiḥ (f. nom. sg.) power (see II:6) [end of TP6 cpd.]

iti (ind.) thus

The return to the origin of the *guṇas*, emptied of their purpose for *puruṣa*, is *kaivalyam*, the steadfastness in own form, and the power of higher awareness.

This concluding *sūtra* completes the definition of yoga as an embodied experience given in I:3: "Then there is abiding in the seer's own form."

Bibliography of Translations Consulted

Āranya, Swāmi Hariharānanda. *Yoga Philosophy of Patañjali: Containing His Yoga Aphorisms with Vyāsa's Commentary in Sanskrit and a Translation with Annotations Including Many Suggestions for the Practice of Yoga.* Rendered into English by P.N. Mukherji. Albany: State University of New York Press, 1983. First published in English by Calcutta University Press in 1963.

Baba, Bangali. *Yogasūtra of Patañjali with the Commentary of Vyāsa, Translated from Sanskrit into English with Copious Notes.* Delhi: Motilal Banarsidass, 1976.

Ballantyne, J.R. and Govind Sastry Deva, trs. *Yogasūtras of Patañjli* (sic) *with Bhojavṛtti called Rājamārtaṇḍa.* Akay Book Corporation, 1980. First published in the *Pandit,* 1852.

Dvivedi, M.N. *The Yoga-sūtras of Patañjali.* Revised edition. Delhi: Sri Satguru Publications, 1980. First published in Madras, 1890.

Feuerstein, Georg. *The Yoga-sūtra of Patañjali: A New Translation and Commentary.* Folkestone, Kent: Wm. Dawson & Sons, 1979.

Ghosh, Shyam. *The Original Yoga as Expounded in Śiva-samhitā, Gheraṇḍa-samhitā and Patañjala Yoga-sūtra.* New Delhi: Munshiram Manoharlal, 1980.

Jyotir Maya Nanda, Swāmi. *Raja Yoga Sūtras.* Miami, Florida: Yoga Research Foundation, 1978.

Prasāda, Rama. *Patañjali's Yoga Sūtras with the Commentary of Vyāsa and the Gloss of Vāchaspati Miśra.* New Delhi: Oriental Books Reprint Corporation. First published in 1912 by Panini Office, Allahabad.

Rukmani, T.S. *Yogavārttika of Vijñāna-bhikṣu: Text with English translation and critical notes along with the text and English translation of the Patañjala Yogasūtras and Vyāsabhāṣya. Volume I: Samādhipāda.* New Delhi: Munshiram Manoharlal, 1981.

Taimni, I.K. *The Science of Yoga: the Yogasūtras of Patañjali in Sanskrit with transliteration in Roman, translation in English and commentary.* Wheaton, Illinois: The Theosophical Publishing House, 1961.

Vivekananda, Swāmi. *Rāja Yoga.* Revised edition. New York: Ramakrisha-Vivekananda Center, 1975.

Woods, James Houghton. *The Yoga-System of Patañjali or the Ancient Hindu Doctrine of Concentration of Mind Embracing the Mnemonic Rules, Called Yoga-Sūtras, of Patañjali and the Comment, Called Yoga-bhāshya, Attributed to Veda-Vyāsa and the Explanation, Called Tattva-vāicāradī, of Vācha-spatimiśra.* Delhi: Motilal Banarsidass, 1977. First published by Harvard University Press, 1914.

Yardi, M.R. *The Yoga of Patañjali with an Introduction, Sanskrit Text of the Yogasūtras, English Translation and Notes.* Poona: Bhandarkar Oriental Research Institutue, 1979.

INDEX OF SANSKRIT TERMS

khyāti i.16; ii.26, 28; iii.49; iv.29
gati ii.49; iii.28
gamana iii.42
guna i.16; ii.15, 19; iv.13, 32, 34
guru i.26
grahaṇa i.41; iii.47
grahītṛ i.41
grāhya i.41; iii.21
ca i.29, 44, 45; ii.2, 15, 41, 53; iii.20, 22, 38, 39, 42, 45, 48, 49, 54; iv.10, 16, 20, 21
cakra iii.29
cakṣus iii.21
caturtha ii.51
candra iii.27
citi iv.22; iv.34
citta i.2, 30, 33, 37; ii.54, iii.1, 9, 11, 12, 19, 34, 38; iv.4, 5, 15, 16, 17, 18, 21, 23, 26
citra iv.24
cetanā i.29
chidra iv.27
ja i.50; iii.52, 54; iv.1, 6
janman ii, 12, 39; iv.1
japa i.28
jaya ii.41; iii.5, 39, 40, 44, 47, 48
jala iii.48
javitva iii.48
jāti ii.13, 31; iii.18; iii.53; iv.2, 9
jāyante iii.36
jugupsā ii.40
jña i.25
jñāta iv.17, 18
jñātṛtva iii.49
jñāna i.8, 9, 38, 42; ii.28; iii.16, 17, 18, 19, 22, 25, 26, 27, 28, 35, 52, 54; iv.31
jñeya iv.31
jyotiṣmati i.36
jyotis iii.32
jvalana iii.40
tatas i.22; i.29; ii.48, 52, 55; iii.12, 36, 45, 48, 53; iv.3, 43
tattva i.32; iv.14
tatra i.13, 42, 48; i.25; iii.2, iv.6
tathā ii.9
tad i.12, 16, 32; ii. 2, 11, 13, 16, 22, 25; iii.3, 5, 8, 20, 21, 50; iv.8, 11, 16, 17, 18, 19, 22, 24, 27
tadā i.3; iv.26, 31; iv.16
tanu ii.4
tantra iv.16
tapas ii.1, 32, 43; iv.1
tayoḥ iv.15
tasmin ii.49
tasya i.27, 51; ii.24, 27; iii.6, 10, 20
tā i.46
tāpa ii.15
tāraka iii.54
tārā iii.27
tāsām iv.10
tīvra i.21
tu i.41; iv.3
tulya ii.12, 53
tūla iii.42
te i.30; ii.10, 14; iii.37; iv.13
tyāga ii.35
traya iii.4, 7, 16
trividha iv.7
darśana i.30;ii.6, 41; iii.32

vrtti i.2, 4, 5, 10, 41; ii.11; iii.43; iv.18
vedanā iii.36
vedanīya ii.12
vaitṛṣṇya i.14
vaira ii.35
vairāgya i.12, 15; iii.50
vaiśāradya i.47
vyakta iv.13
vyavahita iii.25; iv.9
vyākhyātā i.44; iii.13
vyādhi i.30
vyutthāna iii.9, 37
vyūha iii.27, 29
vrata ii.31
śakti ii.6, 23, 34; iii.21
śabda i.9, 42; iii.17
śarīra iii.38
śānta iii.12,14
śīla ii.18
śuci ii.5
śuddha ii.20
śuddhi ii.31; iii.55
śūnya i.9; i.43; iii.3; iv.34
śeṣa i.18
śaithilya ii.47; iii.38
śauca ii.32, 40
śraddhā i.20
śrāvaṇa iii.36
śruta i.49
śrotra iii.41
śvāsa i.31; ii.49
sa i.14
saṃyama iii.4, 16, 17, 21, 22, 26, 35, 41, 42, 44, 47, 52
saṃyoga ii.17, 23, 25
saṃvid iii.34
saṃvega i.21
saṃvedana ii.38; iv.22
saṃśaya i.30
saṃskāra i.18, 50; ii.15; iii.9, 10, 18; iv.9, 27
saṃhatya iv.24
saṃhananatva iii.46
saṃkara iii.17; iv.21
saṃkīrna i.42
samkhyā ii.50
saṅga iii.51
saṃgrhītatva iv.11
saṃjñā i.15
sati ii.13; ii.49
satkāra i.14
sattva i.41; iii.35, 49, 55
satya ii.30, 36
sadā iv.18
saṃtoṣa ii.32, 42
saṃnidhi ii.35
saptadhā ii.27
sabīja i.46
samaya ii.31; iv.20
samādhi i.20, 46, 51; ii.2, 29, 45; iii.3, 11, 37; iv.1, 29
samāna iii.40
samāpatti i.41, 42; ii.47; iii.42
samāpti iv.32
saṃpad iii.45, 46
saṃprajñāta i.17
saṃprayoga ii.44
saṃbandha ii.41.42
sambodha ii.39
sarva i.25, 51; ii.15, 31, 37; iii.11, 17, 33, 49, 54; iv.23, 31